Twayne's United States Authors Series

SYLVIA E. BOWMAN, *Editor*

INDIANA UNIVERSITY

Marc Connelly

MARC CONNELLY

By PAUL T. NOLAN

University of Southwestern Louisiana

 149

Twayne Publishers, Inc.   ::   New York

FOR PEGGY

Preface

THIS BOOK is likely to be a disappointment to the millions of people who know Marc Connelly as a public figure and to the thousands who know him as a personal friend. Both in his public performances—as writer, actor, television guest, and campus lecturer—and in his private associations, Mr. Connelly is the perfect companion—witty, charming, knowledgeable, and compassionate.

For over fifty years as a public man-of-letters, he has entertained millions with a display of talents that cover almost the entire range of the theatrical arts. He is, of course, the author of *The Green Pastures,* a work that Alexander Woollcott once called "the finest American play ever written." But he is more than a one-play author. With George S. Kaufman he wrote a series of comedies—including *Merton of the Movies* and *Beggar on Horseback*—that created a style in sophisticated American comedy which has become the standard for Broadway.

There are few arts in the theater that Mr. Connelly has not practiced with distinction. As a director, he won special acclaim for such work as his staging of his own *The Green Pastures* and of Arthur Kober's *Having Wonderful Time.* As an actor, he can include among his credits the role of the Stage Manager in both New York and London productions of *Our Town.* And he has, at one time or another, been a play doctor, lyricist, musical-comedy writer, promotion man, drama teacher, and discoverer of talent.

Nor has the theater exhausted his talents. He was one of the charter members of the Vicious Circle of the Algonquin Hotel, a group of wits that included half of the quotable men and women in New York during the 1920's—F. P. Adams, Heywood Broun, Alexander Woollcott, George S. Kaufman, Robert Benchley, Dorothy Parker, and Edna Ferber, to select merely some of the still-known personalities whose lives and careers have become part of the Connelly story.

He is the author of a novel, *Souvenir from Qam;* of a dozen short stories, including one that won an O. Henry award for fiction; and of various essays on contemporary society, the theater, travel, and his own experiences. Moreover, with all his claims as a man-of-letters, Marc Connelly may be that rare literary man who is even more loved and admired for himself than for his work. From 1920, when he and Kaufman first came to success with *Dulcy,* through the present year, Mr. Connelly has been a favorite subject of those journalists—like Franklin P. Adams in the 1920's and Leonard Lyons in the 1960's—who chronicle the lives of "interesting" people, not for their scandalous behavior, but for their witty observations, their humane interests, their wide knowledge of the history and practice of the literary arts. It would be easy to compile a long book of the praise given him; however, it might be difficult to pad out even a short essay of personal criticism.

Anyone who has seen Marc Connelly perform on a college campus in recent years can easily understand his personal attraction. Now in his mid-seventies, he walks onto a bare stage and turns it into live theater. He is everything that students want in an academic performer—well-informed, entertaining, talented; and, above all else, he is a man of good intentions and courage. Everything about him communicates a knowledge and love of theater, a respect and fondness for man.

This Marc Connelly—who can rise before seven in the morning for a stroll and then still hate to leave a party at two the following morning—is a remarkable man. To spend even an hour in his company is to realize that he is one of the "great talkers" of our time, a man that John Mason Brown once commented could be "out-talked" only by George Bernard Shaw. In an earlier draft of this book, a considerable amount of attention was given to Connelly's contributions to the oral arts—his droll stories, his pranks, his spoken wit. In the process, unfortunately, the subject of this book, Connelly's written works, was somewhat neglected.

While it is true that Connelly, the man, is a rare individual, one whose personality has enriched many lives, it is equally true that his plays, like *The Green Pastures, Merton of the Movies, Beggar on Horseback,* and *The Wisdom Tooth,* are worth serious attention for their own merits. At the present time, they have not received this attention. This work, for example, is the first in which anyone has even examined all of Mr. Connelly's plays —the unpublished ones as well as the published. A survey of the annual *PMLA Bibliography* for the past fifty years reveals, in fact, that, except for *The Green Pastures,* not a single one of Mr. Connelly's works has been the subject of a formal academic study; and there are only four entries for *The Green Pastures,* including a new edition.

Part of the reason for this neglect is that until recently academic critics did not give much attention to any modern American playwright, except Eugene O'Neill. Connelly's works, moreover, have not been easily available. Only a few of his full-length plays—*Dulcy, To the Ladies!, Merton of the Movies, Beggar on Horseback, The Wisdom Tooth,* and *The Green Pastures* —have ever been published in their entirety. This book, in fact, was made possible only because Mr. Connelly allowed me to use the copyright manuscripts of all his works, including eighteen unpublished plays.

This study, then, attempts to do two things primarily: first, to give evidence that many of Mr. Connelly's works are worth serious attention; and, second, to offer in one place some account of all these works. In both of these aims, this book, while claiming to be "a first," makes no pretense of being "the final" word. As literary criticism, the analyses of the separate works are generally limited to those works that the reader will find available in print. With some of the unpublished plays, however, especially those that were given full-scale professional productions, I have not only given brief accounts, but I have also attempted to indicate some of the critical problems. The focus, nonetheless, is on those works that the reader has already seen, or may see, especially those that are published.

No attempt has been made to establish a central thesis or to argue for any single key that will unlock all of Mr. Connelly's work, much of which was done in collaboration, some on assignment. It is true, of course, that all of his works are consistent with a single point of view—that of the literate, civilized, humane man. It is unlikely, however, that they fit into any single pattern. It is true that there are "problems" with which many of his works deal—the search for paradise, for example; the affirmation of personal integrity through an act of intellectual courage; the individual's attempt to defend himself against outside deception and internal fears. It is true, too, that Connelly "characters" appear in more than one play—Kenneth Mercer and various Bemises, for examples. It does not, however, seem profitable in an introductory work of this nature to subordinate the rich variety of patterns and problems for the purpose of supporting a single thesis.

This study follows a chronological order, dividing the constant flow of an active life into little islands of written works— early works, works with Kaufman, and the like. Such a division, to be sure, is largely mechanical; but the biographer-critic dealing with so many works about which there is so little general knowledge must, to some degree, serve as a curator, keeping the exhibits in the gallery in order.

This is, therefore, a book of literary facts and, it is hoped, critical challenges. Through neglect, ignorance, apathy, and availability problems, students of American literature are in danger of losing some valuable works; and it is a loss that we cannot afford.

AFTER THE FACT: *A Postscript*

While this book was in press, Mr. Connelly's *Voices Offstage: A Book of Memoirs* (New York: Holt, Rinehart & Winston, Inc., 1968) was published. This new work by Marc Connelly is important not only as the most complete account of his literary career, but also because of its own merits as literature, an added demonstration that biographers and critics concerned with Marc Connelly are watching an artist in action, not one in repose.

PAUL T. NOLAN

University of Southwestern Louisiana

Acknowledgments

THIS BOOK owes much to its subject, Marc Connelly. Mr. Connelly not only gave me permission to use both his published and unpublished manuscripts, but he has, also, answered all my queries with courtesy, patience, and wit. During the summer and fall of 1966, Mr. Connelly consented to a series of personal interviews and made available to me for examination some of his works-in-progress. Also, he read an early draft of this book; and while I do not wish to suggest that his cooperation and aid make this book the "authorized work," I do wish to acknowledge my considerable debt to him. He corrected a number of errors in the first draft of the book and gave me additional information not available in any printed source. Any claim this book has to completeness is based entirely on Mr. Connelly's generosity.

Special thanks are due also to Paul A. Thibodeaux of the Smithsonian Institution, to Kenneth B. Toombs of the Dupré Library at the University of Southwestern Louisiana, to Miss Martha Calvert, to Mrs. Woodene Merriman of the McKeesport, Pennsylvania, *Daily News,* and to Miss Susan T. Secor of the Carnegie Library of Pittsburgh for their aid in the location of materials.

I am grateful, too, to my student assistant, Miss Ruth Moran, and to Mrs. Jo Denham, and to the administration of the University of Southwestern Louisiana for material aid and comfort, especially to Dr. Mary E. Dichmann and Dr. Lewis T. Graham.

Finally, I am grateful to my wife for her sensible criticism and her care in helping me to prepare the manuscript for publication.

Contents

Chronology

1890   Born December 13, in McKeesport, Pennsylvania, Marcus Cook Connelly, the first son of Patrick Joseph and Mabel Cook Connelly.

1897   Sees his first stage play, Rostand's *Cyrano de Bergerac* with Richard Mansfield.

1902   Enters Trinity Hall, a private school in Washington, Pennsylvania. Father dies.

1907   Leaves school to begin writing career in Pittsburgh.

1908– Reporter and drama critic for Pittsburgh newspapers.
1915

1913   Sells lyrics for a musical, *The Lady of Luzon*.

1915   Moves to New York for production of his first play, *The Amber Empress*. (This play was later titled *The Amber Princess*.)

1916   *Amber Empress* runs for twenty-five performances at Globe Theatre.

1916– Meets George S. Kaufman, writes for newspapers, works
1920   for theater managers, does free-lance writing.

1921   Writes *Dulcy* with Kaufman. Produced and published.

1922   Writes *To the Ladies!*, *West of Pittsburgh,* and *Merton of the Movies* with Kaufman. All three produced.

1923   *West of Pittsburgh* revised as *Little Old Millersville* and produced as *The Deep Tangled Wildwood*. *Helen of Troy, N.Y.,* a musical written with Kaufman, produced.

1924   *Beggar on Horseback,* a play, and *Be Yourself,* a musical, both written with Kaufman, produced.

1925   Writes *How's the King?,* a musical. Named to editorial board of *The New Yorker*. Writes *The Wisdom Tooth*.

1926   *The Wisdom Tooth* opens in New York and is published in abridged form in *Best Plays of 1925–26*. *Ex Cathedra* published in *Theatre Arts Monthly* and *The Traveller* in *The New Yorker*.

1927   *How's the King?* produced. *The Wild Man of Borneo* (with Herman J. Mankiewicz) has short run in New York.

1929   Writes *The Green Pastures*. Copyrights *The Bridegroom, The Burglar, The Suitor,* and *The Uncle*—all produced as film shorts by RKO–Radio Pictures, with Connelly playing the leads.

1930   Wins Pulitzer Prize for drama for *The Green Pastures,* and an O. Henry award for the short story for "Coroner's Inquest." Stages William Bolitho's *Overture, 1920.* Marries Hollywood actress, Madeline Hurlock, October 4.

1931   *The Green Pastures* continues its original New York run, eventually to total six hundred forty performances. *The Unemployed Ghost* produced as film short.

1932   Writes *Service,* a one-act play, with Kaufman.

1933–   Divides time between Hollywood and New York. Writes
1944   screenplays for *Cradle Song* (1933); *Captains Courageous* (1937); *I Married a Witch* (1942); and *Reunion* (1942).

1934   *The Farmer Takes a Wife,* written with Frank B. Elser, has successful New York run. *The Survey,* a short skit, published in *The New Yorker*.

1935   *The Green Pastures* returns to New York for run of seventy-three performances. Connelly divorced by wife.

1936   Produces *Till the Cows Come Home* at the St. Martin's Theatre in London. Writes screenplay for, and directs, *The Green Pastures* for Warner Brothers.

1937   Produces, directs, and finances Arthur Kober's *Having Wonderful Time* in New York.

1938   Helps rewrite Arnold Sundgaard's *Everywhere I Roam,* produces it, and directs it for New York run. Copyrights *The Land of the Living*.

1939   Stages *The Happiest Days. The Traveler* published in play form.

1941 *The Mole on Lincoln's Cheek,* a radio play, broadcast and published.

1942 Writes and stages *The Flowers of Virtue* in New York.

1944 Plays role of Stage Manager in New York production of *Our Town.*

1945 With Jean Dalrymple, stages *Hope for the Best* in New York.

1946 Plays role of Stage Manager in London production of *Our Town.*

1947 Appointed playwriting professor at Yale University.

1948 Writes and stages *A Story for Strangers* in New York.

1951 *The Green Pastures* revived in New York for short run. Appointed United States Commissioner to United Nations Educational, Scientific, and Cultural Organization.

1952 Copyrights *Rehearsal for the Feast* (a revised version of *Ex Cathedra*) and *There Are Two Points* (a revision of *The Land of the Living*). Resigns from Yale faculty.

1953 President of National Institute of Arts and Letters.

1954 Two autobiographical sketches in *The New Yorker.* Copyrights *The Riddle,* a motion picture play.

1958 Plays role in *The Tall Story. Hunter's Moon (There Are Two Points)* directed by Connelly for London performance.

1959 Repeats stage role in *The Tall Story* for motion picture production. *The Green Pastures,* adapted by Connelly, produced on television, March 23.

1960 Serves with Thornton Wilder as advisor for Equity Theatre Library.

1961 Copyrights *The Portable Yenberry,* a full-length comedy.

1962 *The Portable Yenberry,* directed by Connelly, given at Purdue University, Indiana, for eight performances.

1965 *A Souvenir from Qam,* Connelly's first novel, published.

1966– Public lectures, travel, acting, and writing continue.
1968 Novel, musical comedy, memoirs, and travel pieces in progress.

Marc Connelly

CHAPTER 1

Marcus Cook Connelly:
To the Manner Born

IF MARCUS COOK CONNELLY had not eventually become a playwright, actor, director, or producer, his parents would have had some right to be surprised. Although during his first years in New York, Broadway wits tried to make humor of the fact that he was born in the "West"—McKeesport, Pennsylvania,[1] twenty miles west of Pittsburgh—Connelly grew up in a theatrical tradition that is everywhere present in his work. If critics complain that he is sometimes sentimental, romantic, "charming," he might justly answer that he is the product of his environment and heritage. In an essay, published in 1954,[2] a few days after his sixty-fourth birthday, Connelly recalled the days of his youth. "By my standards," he wrote, "McKeesport was a metropolis unlimited in area and population," a Mark Twain kind of town. But, if there is something of the Tom Sawyer about his youth, it was Tom with shiny shoes and a pass to the theater.

I *The Theatrical Connellys*

The Connelly family settled in Pennsylvania in the mid-nineteenth century when Marc's grandfather came to the United States as an emigrant from Ireland. By the time Marc's father, Patrick Joseph, had reached his young manhood, the Connellys had spread themselves throughout the western Pennsylvania area. During his youth, Marc wrote, ". . . my father's parents, his married sister, and numerous other relatives were in nearby communities."[3] His father, who was born in Pittsburgh, had a reputation as a singer; and he was encouraged by his friends and relatives to go on the stage. In the mid-1880's, when he was twenty years old, Joseph followed this advice and left home with a touring company.

A year later, a seasoned veteran of the road, he found a job with Steele MacKaye as an assistant manager of the Lyceum Theatre in New York. In 1886, the ownership of the theater changed hands; and Joseph Connelly returned to the road, playing juvenile leads with a travelling company. Later that year, he was in Boston with a resident company; and there he met Mabel Fowler Cook, the eighteen-year-old daughter of Marcus Carlin Cook, an affluent merchant and a friend of Henry Cabot Lodge. The Cook family, Marc has written, did not approve of actors, "particularly one whose parents had been Irish immigrants. . . ."[4] The Cooks were Episcopalians, and the Connellys were Catholics. When Joseph and Mabel eloped, therefore, the marriage was viewed with considerable displeasure by her family. Mabel, however, seems not to have been intimidated by her parents' disapproval. She not only married an actor and toured the country with him, but she also joined him as a performer on the stage.

Joseph, too, had family problems at home. The Connellys, according to Marc, were dismayed that Joseph had married an English girl outside their faith. Both families, however, were long distances away; and the acting Connellys flourished. In 1888, a daughter was born to them, and the Connellys became a travelling trio.

In the winter of 1888–89, the Connellys with their infant daughter were touring the Midwest. One night in Duluth, Minnesota, the baby became ill with pneumonia; and, before medical help could be found, the child died. "Their anguish," Marc wrote, "was intensified by self-reproach for having subjected her to the hazards of travel. They wanted another child; so they quit the stage and settled in McKeesport. I was born there a year later."[5]

II *Growing Up in McKeesport*

From the day of his birth, December 13, 1890, until he left McKeesport in 1907 to begin his career as a professional writer,

Marc seems to have led a most pleasant life. His parents were leaders in their community, and they gave him all the affection that a healthy growing boy could reasonably stand. The bond of affection between Marc and his mother lasted throughout her life, and one might reasonably assume that the source for his pleasant heroines rests in his relationship with her. It was to her that he dedicated *The Green Pastures.*

A few years after Marc's birth, around 1893, Joseph, who had been operating a restaurant, took over the management of the White Hotel, "near the Baltimore and Ohio Depot" in McKeesport.[6] The family lived in the hotel, and Marc divided his career ambitions between his desires to be an actor like his father or an engineer on the railroad.[7] The elder Connelly had not only been an actor, but a theater manager and director for some of the more popular figures in the American theater, including Steele MacKaye and Richard Mansfield. The White Hotel became the stopping place for road companies playing the western Pennsylvania area, and the young Marc met many of the best-known actors and actresses of the time.

Years later, when he turned actor to do the role of the Stage Manager in *Our Town,* he told a reporter that he had learned his craft studying under Robert Mantell, Minnie Maddern Fiske, and Richard Mansfield, watching them when they were guests in his father's hotel and practicing their movements in front of the mirror. "I started acting in my own plays at the age of eight in my father's hotel . . . ," he told Bob Thomas in an interview in 1959. "My father had been an actor, and all the theatrical people stayed there. You may think this is an ordinary hand [showing Thomas his hand], but that delivered a glass of grape juice to Buffalo Bill Cody. He was on the wagon then."[8]

When Marc was seven, his parents took him to Pittsburgh for his first visit to a professional theater. Richard Mansfield was playing Rostand's *Cyrano de Bergerac.* The train from McKeesport was slow, and the Connellys did not arrive until the first act was in progress. Marc did not at first understand that he was watching a play. He was, in fact, so restless that his father had to tell him to pay attention. Then he found himself "involved" in the play. He had, he said later, confused the theater with a church, but that confusion led him to a kind of truth about the theater that he has retained all of his life.

"Since then," he wrote of that first experience, "the stage ... [has] become familiar to me ... [but] going to the theatre is [still] like going to an unusual church where the spirit is nourished in mysterious ways, and pure magic may occur at any time." The "pure magic" of that first experience was made especially memorable by an unusual occurrence. Mansfield saw his friends, the Connellys, enter the theater late. He knew this was Marc's first play, and he asked the audience for its indulgence to allow him to repeat the first act for his good friends. The audience approved, and Marc saw the complete play without interruption.[9]

When Marc returned home after that experience, he knew he had found his place in life. A few years later, by the age of eleven, "Connelly was already a veteran playwright, producer, and actor.... He put on numerous plays including 'The Great Counterfitters of New York,' 'The Great Diamond Ring Mistery,' and 'The Great Shipreck or Saved By a Brave Sailer' in his nine-seat theatre on the second floor of his father's hotel in McKeesport, Pa."[10] "I wrote these plays when I was nine years old," Mr. Connelly told me, "and spell the titles correctly."

Theater, to be sure, was only a small part of Marc's life in McKeesport. Most of his time was given to the normal daily routine of small-town life—school, play, and church. He joined his mother's church and attended services in St. Stephen's Protestant Episcopal Church, singing in the choir and joining the Junior Brotherhood of St. Andrew.[11] When he was twelve, in 1902, Marc enrolled at Trinity Hall in nearby Washington, Pennsylvania. That same year his father died, and with that death, in many respects, Marc's life as a small-town boy ended. His mother ran the White Hotel for a few years, but finally lost it in a depression. Marc remained, until he was seventeen, in Trinity Hall, which he later described as "an outrageous, small hybrid school ... which supposedly was founded by General Grant. It was a combination of learning and military academy."[12] In 1907 he left school to go to Pittsburgh to begin his career with a newspaper. "I was hell-bent on being a writer," he said.[13]

III *With the Pittsburgh Newspapers*

Connelly's first newspaper job was with the Pittsburgh *Sun.* "... I got a job ... as a classified ad collector through collusion," he said. "I knew the daughter of the editor. The job paid $22 a week but was upped to $28 when I began writing a column filled with worldly philosophy (at age 17?) ."[14] George Kaufman, with whom Connelly was to collaborate on their first successful plays, also started his writing career on the Pittsburgh newspapers, but he had left there for a position with Munsey's Washington *Times* shortly before Connelly arrived in Pittsburgh, and the two did not meet until Connelly went to New York several years later.[15]

As a reporter and assistant drama critic, Connelly spent almost eight years in Pittsburgh, moving from the *Sun* to the *Dispatch* and then, finally, to the *Gazette Times,* for which he wrote play reviews, news stories, and a humor column—work which demonstrates little more than his general competence as a newspaper reporter and likeable versifier.

IV Jots and Tittles

In some of his feature articles, like the one he wrote about German children in 1915, there are some suggestions that Connelly was probably a little more aware of the human problem than was the average newspaper man. During 1915, when Americans, according to Connelly, had only a spectator interest in the war—"Today the Allies have done so and so. The Germans have accomplished this and that"—young Marc observed that there was little real understanding of the future the war would bring because the average American ". . . does not hear the children of Europe."[16] His analysis of letters the children were sending to German-American children in Pittsburgh forecasts, in some general respects, the post-war Germany that would listen to Hitler.

Connelly, of course, was not primarily concerned with international news in those years before the United States' entry into the war. He was, rather, a city reporter, commenting upon such local matters as new methods of growing corn and cabbage;[17] and a humorous columnist, the author of a series of verse-and-prose comments, *Jots and Tittles.* The verse he wrote demonstrates his aversion to war, a distaste for public speaking, a good-natured belief in the superiority of women, and a fondness for doggerel. In one verse, for example, he points to the American's failure to understand war in terms of human suffering:

I notice that the czar has lost
  Two hundred thousand heroes,
I see they're bawling one another
  Out for being Neroes,
It's sickening to see how men
  Such bloody fame can covet.
Put on your hat and let's go see
  The movie version of it.[18]

Such verses as these, Mr. Connelly told me recently, "are infantile. Tennyson wrote much better when he was fourteen in a poem that begins 'Ten thousand thousand myriadoms martially arrayed.' This [verse] must have been a contribution because I'm damned if I could think I had written anything as bad as that."

His main interest, as a matter of fact, was in the theater. In 1913, he sold some lyrics for a new musical, *The Lady of Luzon,* by A. W. Birdsall and Joseph Parenteau. It was performed for the Pittsburgh Athletic Club and was seen by "a steel tycoon who wanted to be a Broadway angel." When *The Lady of Luzon* went to New York in 1915, for a short, uneventful run, the "tycoon" suggested that Connelly do the book and lyrics for an operetta. Connelly then wrote *The Amber Princess,* with music by Parenteau.[19]

V *Broadway Opening*

The Amber Princess opened September 9, 1917, in New York; ran for fifteen performances; and folded. "I wasn't disappointed," Mr. Connelly told me. "I was mad." But he did not take the failure personally. "It was produced in New York after it had been so rewritten by every librettist in town that the lyrics of one song were all that remained of my book." Whenever Mr. Connelly speaks of his move to New York, he always comments that, after the failure of *The Amber Princess,* he "lacked money to go home, so stayed in New York."[20] Connelly, as a matter of fact, had copyrighted the play from New York, but he had given his Pittsburgh address. Obviously, however, once he had a play on Broadway, he knew that his future was in New York, then the only place in America for anyone serious about writing for the stage.

With the failure of *The Amber Princess,* Connelly began a half-decade of free-lance writing, theatrical odd jobs, and playwriting failures. These were the "lean years," as Walter Prichard Eaton called them, "in which Marc was able to keep his figure, but not his hair." Perhaps his most spectacular failure was as the press agent for a musical comedy, *Honeydew.* The producer, Joe Weber, had invested a great deal of money in the promotion of the play which was to open at the Casino Theatre in·the fall of 1920. When Connelly forgot the opening night announcements, Weber fired him. As Eaton comments, *Honeydew* ". . . was no melon for Marc."[21] Connelly's playwriting during these years included work with a musical comedy called *Follow the Girl* and another musical, probably an adaptation of *Ermine.* "The total run of these operas, if laid end to end would reach exactly to Cain's storehouse—and did," Eaton wrote of them.[22]

About the time that he lost his job with *Honeydew,* Connelly met Kaufman. Both had left out-of-town newspaper jobs for a chance at Broadway, and, after five years, both had little to show for their work except experience. Kaufman, who was married, did have a full-time job as an assistant dramatic critic for the New York *Times,* a position he continued to hold for several years after he was an established playwright. Connelly had hopes.

There was obviously a great deal of fondness and respect between the two men from the beginning of their relationship. Although their collaborations ended after five years, their friendship and mutual support continued for life. In 1951, for example, Connelly told Tex McCrary and Jinx Falkenburg a story about Kaufman that illustrates the nature of Connelly's admiration. "George Kaufman," he told them, "gave us an example of that [courage]. About 1918, I ran into him in the lobby of the Knickerbocker Theater, which, for a relatively brief period, housed a play George co-authored called 'Someone in the House.' There was a flu epidemic at the time—all the newspapers were warning readers to 'AVOID CROWDS'—and business was bad, very bad. George looked glummer than usual that evening, not so much because the play wasn't going well, but because his producer refused to let him run an inspired advertisement on the theatrical pages. Kaufman's ad—'AVOID CROWDS—SEE "SOMEONE IN THE HOUSE"!!' "[23]

By 1920, when Connelly started his collaborations with Kaufman, he was thirty years old and had little fame or fortune to show for his thirteen years of writing. If all that he had written during that time were now collected, it would make a volume of some size and would include parts of plays, lyrics for musicals, newspaper columns and popular essays; but such a collection would be of doubtful literary value. The real worth of these years, aside from the fact that they led Connelly to New York and to a meeting with Kaufman, rests on the use to which Connelly has put his private experiences in his plays and, more recently, in his autobiographical essays. Professor Eaton suggests that in such early comedies as *Beggar on Horseback* and *The Wisdom Tooth,* Connelly drew on this autobiographical material for parts of the plays.[24] Quite obviously, the "Little Old Millersville," that town "West of Pittsburgh" that he created for *The Deep Tangled Wildwood,* owes a great deal to McKeesport.

Although this book is not concerned with Mr. Connelly's personal life, anyone evaluating the intent of his comedy needs to be aware that—in spite of a great deal of good fortune—he has not been a stranger to tragedy and hardship. His father died when Marc was a child; he left school at seventeen, in part to support his mother; he was stranded in New York with a failure in his twenties; and he was, in his own terms "without prospects" when he was thirty. Connelly seems, however, to have been born with the comic spirit. He has always had a comic view of life.

Bernard K. Schilling, in defining the character of the comic artist, although not mentioning Connelly, gives a description that would fit him. The comic artist, writes Schilling, is a man with a "sense of the richness of life"; and he is willing to participate in it, accepting the full "responsibility of being human." He has "a certain discernment"—the result of his "intelligence, his wit, and his culture"—which gives him "an ability to see man as incongruously different from what he should be. . . ."[25]

Connelly's "intelligence, his wit, and his culture" are such that in using the events of his life as the "raw material" for his works, he has made them evidence both of the foolishness and glory of man; and he has never forgotten that he is part of that man. Certain of the decency and dignity of man, he has in his works examined the ludicrous positions in which man, including Marc Connelly, often finds himself. Sometimes he is saddened;

more often he is amused and hopeful. Always he accepts the full "responsibility of being human."

"I have gone through the world," Mr. Connelly said recently, "to confirm the feeling that theater is primarily a place of enlightenment. It's a mirror in which man has seen his faults and sometimes had the sense to correct them."[26]

Connelly's lyrics for one of his songs in *Lady of Luzon* label "Sleepy Manila" an "Eden of dreams."[27] Obviously, we should not place much weight upon his use of this single cliché in an early work. Throughout his life, however, Connelly has returned again and again to the idea of Eden. He has always been an artist with a hankering for "paradise" and a fundamental belief that reason, good humor, and trust are the means of achieving it.

If Connelly's early work gives but little evidence of the artistry and sense of dedication needed to write *The Green Pastures,* it is yet clear in all his work that everything in his nature and environment helped to mold the kind of man who would have the courage and ambition to try such a play. From his first newspaper work to his most current work-in-progress, Connelly has given a view of life that is hopeful and modest, comic and tolerant. He has brought to his literary life the sense of dedication of his New England ancestors, the sense of adventure of his Irish forebears, and the wonderful insight of a father and mother who knew how to carve a happy marriage from the union of the two.

CHAPTER 2

Life with George S. Kaufman

MARC CONNELLY's career as a collaborator with George S. Kaufman lasted about five years, from 1920 to 1924. During this time, the two wrote at least four plays of permanent interest in the history of American drama: *Dulcy, To the Ladies!, Merton of the Movies,* and *Beggar on Horseback.* They wrote several others, some successful and some failures at the box office—including *The Deep Tangled Wildwood; Helen of Troy, N. Y.;* and *Be Yourself*—which are occasionally mentioned in theater histories, but are never seen or read.[1]

By the standards of some modern theater critics, the Connelly-Kaufman plays are "quaint" and "dated," save perhaps for *Beggar on Horseback,* which Joseph Mersand as late as 1964 was still calling "one of the first great satires on American big business."[2] These plays, to be sure, have ingredients that offend modern critical biases. They are all concerned with the pursuit of fame, fortune, and love; they are all "hopeful" plays. If, however, some critics are now convinced that modern life is better mirrored in Samuel Beckett's *Endgame,* Edward Albee's *Tiny Alice,* or Arthur Miller's *After the Fall,* and if they find the Connelly dialogue a little too "glib," the Kaufman plotting a little too "contrived," and the life that is depicted a little too gay, with too many happy endings, the defenders have an answer. Life *was* glib and gay when these plays were written, and their authors did find happy endings.

Connelly is generally listed as the second half of the Kaufman-Connelly team; and although various theater historians have tried,[3] it is probably a fruitless effort to attempt to isolate Connelly from this union and to deal with him as a separate artist.

Kaufman, himself, commented to one of his later collaborators, Moss Hart, "How the hell would he [a reviewer] or anyone else know who wrote what parts of a play?"[4]

It is not, furthermore, a problem of determining merely what each man brought to each play, but what was given, or suggested to them, by their friends, like Franklin P. Adams, Robert Benchley, Harold Ross, Heywood Broun, Alexander Woollcott, Laurence Stallings, Dorothy Parker, and Edna Ferber, just to mention a few of the Algonquin Round Table wits with whom Kaufman and Connelly came to fame in the first half of the 1920's. Connelly, in fact, has said that the principal reason for their only failure, *The Deep Tangled Wildwood,* was that, in writing that play, they asked for—and accepted—all the advice their friends had to offer.

I   *The Algonquin Wits*

Connelly and Kaufman both had several difficult years before success came. These years in New York, immediately following the war, were, in fact, lean ones for most of the Algonquin group. Indeed, successes were so rare that Herman J. Mankiewicz, George Kaufman's assistant on the *Times* who was later to receive credit for a collaboration with Connelly on *The Wild Man of Borneo,* called the group, ". . . the greatest collection of unsalable wit in America."[5]

It was, at least in part, failure that brought Connelly and this group together. The Algonquin Hotel had a reputation for being "respectful" to theater people and writers—and it had an equally good reputation for serving meals cheaply. For these reasons, a group of writers gathered each day for lunch, to share their wit and their hopes. Several of them had been in service together in France, some of them working on the old *Stars and Stripes.* Most of them had some association with either the daily New York newspapers or such magazines as *Smart Set* and *Life.*

The members of the group, later to be known as the Round Table and the Vicious Circle, did not start as a club. They were, rather, men and women who found pleasure in one another's company, perhaps solace in one another's failures and hope in one another's successes. Among them were Adams, Deems Taylor, Kaufman and Connelly, Benchley, Harold Ross, Broun, Art Samuels, Woollcott, John Peter Toohey, the Pembertons, Bill

Murray, Robert E. Sherwood, John V. A. Weaver, Laurence Stallings, David Wallace, Herman J. Mankiewicz, Dorothy Parker, Jane Grant, Ruth Hale, Beatrice Kaufman (George's wife), Peggy Leach, Margalo Gillmore, Edna Ferber, and Neysa McMein.

It was directly from their association with the Algonquin wits that Connelly and Kaufman's first success came. F. P. Adams, "generally considered the dean of the group," had created a character, Dulcinea, in his newspaper column, "The Conning Tower." He used the character to satirize the dull, cliché-ridden upper-class housewife. Connelly and Kaufman borrowed the character and built their play, *Dulcy,* around her.

II   *The First Success:* Dulcy

It is a little difficult today, in an age when Peter Weiss's *Marat/Sade* and Albee's *Who's Afraid of Virginia Woolf?* have been so successful, to understand the immediate popularity of *Dulcy.* It opened in Indianapolis, moved to Chicago for a successful run, and then was brought to New York on August 13, 1921, to open the season. Burns Mantle selected it as one of the ten plays for his *Best Plays of 1921–1922*;[6] and, when *Dulcy* completed its run, Connelly and Kaufman were the most popular playwriting team on Broadway. Mantle, in selecting *Dulcy* for his anthology, was worried that its subject, the superficiality of the housewife, might be too specialized for a general audience. "Its bromidic heroine," he wrote, "is not easily recognized as an amusing type in all sections, but she is true and furnishes an excellent subject for satiric treatment."[7]

The basic critical objection to *Dulcy*—at least one that might be made upon first examination—is that its action contradicts its theme. Dulcinea, especially as played by Lynn Fontanne, is an amusing portrait of a fatuous woman; but it is doubtful that there is any real satire intended. If the play is to be a criticism of such a woman, the action should support whatever statement is being made about her; but such is not the case. The world of *Dulcy* is not saved *from* this "bromidic" woman, as, for example, Congreve's society in *The Way of the World* is saved from Lady Wishfort. Rather, the world of *Dulcy* is saved *by* her, not in spite of her foibles, but because of them.

[33]

Dulcy, it seems apparent, does not have a critical satiric intent. The "foibles" of the witless are not displayed with any hope of reform but for the sheer pleasure of observing ridiculous behavior. There is, in fact, a quality of tolerance in *Dulcy* that the purposeful satirist cannot afford for his subject, no matter how tolerant he may be of his characters. This tolerance, almost an affection, gives the play its quality.

Dulcy[8] is a conventional three-act situation comedy, set in the living room of Dulcinea Smith's suburban home in Westchester County. The basic action concerns three related episodes in the life of an upper-class young couple, Dulcy and Gordon Smith. The first act, set "Just before dinner on a Friday night," introduces the problems of the various characters; and all these problems are concerned with fame, fortune, and a kind of sexless sentimental love. The second act, "Immediately after dinner," complicates the problems; and the third act, "The following morning," brings the solutions.

The occasion for the gathering of the characters is a week-end party that Dulcy gives for C. Roger Forbes, the second Mrs. Forbes, and Forbes' young daughter, Angela. Forbes is taking over Gordon's jewelry business in a merger, and Dulcy's first problem is to convince him that he should give Gordon more than sixteen and two-thirds of the new business in exchange. "But only sixteen and two-thirds per cent," she complains, "—it's such a funny number, too. I don't see why you couldn't get a nice even number like twenty-five. (*She pauses.*) Or fifty!"

Gordon's problem, which fortunately for him he does not solve, is to keep Dulcy out of his business. He tells her, "I feel that I ought to handle it [the business] alone—in office hours."

Dulcy complicates her problem by her selection of other guests she has invited to help her: a young man suffering from the illusion that he is a multi-millionaire, Schuyler Van Dyck; William Parker, Dulcy's brother, who is in love with Angela; and Vincent Leach, a "scenarist," who is also in love with Angela. For the first two acts, Dulcy's plans to influence Forbes go awry. She arranges a meeting between Mrs. Forbes and Leach so that Leach can help Mrs. Forbes with her screen-writing ambitions. This plan succeeds only in making Forbes jealous of his young second wife and angry at Dulcy. She tells Forbes that Gordon is a busy man with many other projects besides the jewelry business, but this information, instead of impressing Forbes with Gordon's worth, makes him doubt that a part-time partner is worth sixteen and two-thirds percent. She attempts to arrange an elopement between Angela and Leach and succeeds in making Forbes decide to leave the Smith home as quickly as possible and end all relations with Gordon. Even her generous attempt to reform a forger, Henry, into a butler seems to result in another disaster when Henry and a valuable pearl necklace disappear together.

Fortunately for Dulcy and the world of the Smiths, all the characters are innocents and—in spite of their pretensions—generally decent, generally well-intentioned, and all equally witless. Forbes finally agrees to give Smith twenty-five percent of the business; for, despite Dulcy's blundering confession that her young guest is a fraud, Forbes believes that the harmless nut is Schuyler Van Dyck, the millionaire he pretends to be. "I'll admit," Forbes says of Dulcy, "that Mrs. Smith is a clever woman—a very clever woman. (*Smith looks at him wonderingly.*) But it won't work. (*A pause.*) Van Dyck *not* Van Dyck. Hah!"

All of the solutions to the various problems are effected in a like manner. Angela is saved from a hasty marriage to Leach by a hasty marriage to William, Dulcy's brother; and, since "Bill" is an honest "stock broker," rather than "a genius," Forbes is pleased. The butler, Henry, has been completely misjudged. He had taken the necklace for safekeeping; it had been left carelessly about in a house full of strangers. Dulcy, in spite of her success, promises Gordon, "I'll never interfere with your business affairs again."

What pleased audiences about *Dulcy* and gave Kaufman and Connelly popular reputations as satirists is, of course, the dialogue. Professor Arthur Hobson Quinn, who called the play "a clever comedy," maintained that Dulcy's foolishness is set in contrast to the wit of the other characters, notably her brother's.[9] With the exception of William, however, wit in the others is a little difficult to find.

Dulcy is a storehouse of trite expressions, "bromides." "The nicest kind of household" is one in which "anyone can drop in"; "My books are my best friends"; ". . . if a woman is good-looking, no jury on earth will convict her"; and there is "A time and place for everything," according to Dulcy. Leach, as William comments, talks in movie subtitles; and his account of his new movie, *Sin,* is a parody that delighted Quinn. *Sin* is "an extra-super feature, not released on the regular programme!" "It begins—with the setting out—on Noah's Ark," Leach tells the others in a long scene in which he acts out the movie, as Van Dyck plays "Sailing, Sailing" for background music. Tom Sterrett, an "Advertising engineer" and another of Angela's suitors, speaks the jargon of the new breed, a burlesque of the advertising man that had been done earlier in Roi Cooper Megrue and Walter Hackett's *It Pays to Advertise.* Forbes speaks the jargon of the "successful American business man."

There is, however, uncertainty as to whether the dialogue is intended to satirize or merely to identify. Unfortunately for those who would argue for the satiric intent of *Dulcy,* even the stage directions are studded with clichés. Gordon, on first appearance, for example, is described as "an alert young business man with worry just beginning to set on his shoulders"; Sterrett, as a young man with "a snappy style." Joseph Wood Krutch commented that the "satire" of *Dulcy* was new to Broadway, "in a direction more familiar to readers of H. L. Mencken."[10] It was, he argued, "... satire from a point of view rather 'smart' than strictly popular, and local rather than universal in its appeal."[11] Edmond M. Gagey[12] saw in Leach's account of *Sin* critical "satire" of the silent films. John Gassner, in writing of all of the plays by Kaufman and Connelly, concluded: "Their mockery was barbed although they generally withdrew the arrow for the sake of amiability and a full box-office till. Their cynicism was often knowing, their flippancy amusing and at worst just a trifle too empty; only their sentiment, as a rule, was without any sort of merit other than good will."[13]

Which of these judgments a reader now accepts depends, of course, on what service he thinks a play like *Dulcy* should perform. Krutch and Gagey obviously view drama as a part of the running commentary on society; Gassner would like it to be a moral force. From both views, *Dulcy* is less meaningful today than it was forty-five years ago. The value of local "smart talk" is easily diminished with the passing of a generation. As a vehicle for pleasant entertainment, however, *Dulcy* is still competent theater; and, if it has but little to say thematically, its tone still implies a doctrine of tolerance that is of considerable value.

III   *The Second Success:* To the Ladies![14]

Connelly celebrated his success with *Dulcy,* according to Margaret Case Harriman, by buying "a riding habit when the money began to roll in, although he did not as yet own a horse";[15] and immediately he and Kaufman went to work on a second play, *To the Ladies!,* a comedy that might properly be called a companion piece to *Dulcy. To the Ladies!,* which made a "star" of Helen Hayes, also deals with the subject of a wife who tries to help her husband. In this play, however, the husband is the dull fellow; and the wife, unlike Dulcy, is wise, patient, and helpful. Burns Mantle liked *To the Ladies!* but thought *Dulcy* superior to it.[16] Quinn, on the other hand, thought *To the Ladies!* "an improvement upon *Dulcy* because the types are less eccentric and the characters of Leonard and Elsie Beebe achieve reality."[17] Professor Quinn, in fact, selected *To the Ladies!,* which opened in February, 1922, as the best "domestic comedy" of the post-war period. He acknowledged that, for many of his contemporaries, the satire of the public banquet was the chief virtue of the play. He admitted: ". . . that scene is extremely well done"; but he admired the "sentiment" of the play—the same sentiment that Gassner found to be without "any sort of merit"—above the satire.

"A play like *To the Ladies!,*" Quinn wrote, "treating marriage without bitterness, with reticence and with sympathy, is worth a dozen morbid analyses of mismated couples, for it is nearer truth and it creates beauty, and therefore it is better art."[18] Like *Dulcy,* however, *To the Ladies!* is, in one respect, a play about a "mismated couple." In the first play, Connelly and Kaufman mated a sensible man with a foolish woman. In *To the Ladies!*— as if to answer any charges that *Dulcy* was an attack upon the housewife—the husband, Leonard, is a foolish man, and the wife, Elsie, is a wise woman.

Quinn called *To the Ladies!* a "companion piece" to *Dulcy;* and, in some respects, it is the same plot with variations. *Dulcy* is set in an upper-class suburban environment; *To the Ladies!* opens in the middle-class home of Leonard Beebe in Nutley, New Jersey. Both families, however, have the same social aims. Both plays have a set-scene parody; the banquet scene in the second act of *To the Ladies!,* with the speech by Senator Cassidy, performs the same service for this play that Leach's account of *Sin* does for *Dulcy*. In both plays, the husband's career is saved by the interference of the wife.

To the Ladies!, however, makes a positive statement about society in the theme as well as in the action, and the theme and action support each other. Life will be better, the play suggests, when men in business become aware of the importance of women. Just before the curtain falls on the last act, Myrtle Kincaid, the wife of Leonard's employer, is recommending a new appointment to her husband on the basis that the candidate's wife is "... such an able woman."

To the Ladies!, like *Dulcy*, shows that happiness is best achieved through a pleasant marriage and a profitable business career. Leonard, an office worker in Kincaid's piano factory, has been invited to the annual company banquet at which he is to give a short speech. Since this speech will be used to determine whether Leonard or his competitor, Tom Baker, will be promoted, both the Beebes are anxious about it. Leonard, like Gordon in *Dulcy*, is also worried that his wife's interference might hurt his chances. Leonard, however, does not have Gordon's reasons for concern; Elsie is no Dulcy. In the first act, Elsie demonstrates that she is a "superior kind" of woman when she is able to save Leonard's chances with his employer by her honesty and quick thinking. During a visit to the Beebes, Mr. and Mrs. Kincaid discover that Leonard is so deeply in debt that his piano—a Kincaid piano—is being taken back for nonpayment. Elsie quickly explains that Leonard's immediate financial difficulties stem from his ambitions; he borrowed money to buy a grapefruit farm in Florida. Then she wins the support of both Kincaids with a sentimental speech about the hardships of poverty.

Leonard, however, does not learn easily that his wife is his superior. He copies a speech from *Five Hundred Speeches for All Occasions*, which he intends to pass off as his own, in spite of Elsie's warning that he should be original. At the banquet, her wisdom is proven. Baker, Leonard's competitor, speaks first; and his speech is the one Leonard has memorized. Elsie rescues her husband by explaining to the group that Leonard has laryngitis and asks permission to give his speech for him. She wins the support of Mrs. Kincaid, who knows that back of every successful man stands a good woman; and Elsie's speech—full of sentiment and modesty—wins the promotion for Leonard.

A cynical critic, at this point, might wonder about Elsie's reasons for marrying Leonard in the first place; and the last act does nothing to answer such a question. As it opens, Leonard is dictating a letter to his secretary: "As you know, we believe as a general rule women are not as capable as men in business." Again, his world starts to fall apart. Kincaid discovers that Leonard was not the author of the speech and starts to demote him; but Elsie, aided by Mrs. Kincaid, reminds Kincaid, tactfully, that he, too, is little without his wife. And with that piece of *Ladies' Home Companion* philosophy, the play ends.

Although *To the Ladies!* is more sentimental than *Dulcy*, it is not so good-humored. One character in the play, Chester Mullin, has qualities that might have made him a candidate for the Algonquin Round Table. He has imagination, brashness, and daring, but, when he tries to promote a wonderfully fantastic idea for advertising Kincaid pianos, Elsie treats him as a threat to Leonard; and in the last act, his wild hopes shattered, Chester is about ready to settle for being a permanent office boy. The rival of the "hero" in *Dulcy*—Leach, the scenario writer—is last seen chasing the automobile in which the lovers, Angela and William, are eloping, a most apt conclusion in harmony with the short-reel silent films for which Leach writes. In contrast, the rival of the hero in *To the Ladies!*, Baker, takes his farewell, whining that he has been cheated in the speech competition. Dulcy, no matter how temporary her reform, does acknowledge the error of her ways, even though they have worked. Leonard, exposed a dozen times, is as dull and smug when the curtain goes down as he was when it went up.

To the Ladies! in trying to be more—and its action does support its theme, which is not true of *Dulcy*—is less. In the world of *Dulcy*, hallucinations are forgiven if they work, and it is not only the deluded Van Dyck who has them; but the play makes it clear that the success is accidental. In *To the Ladies!*, on the other hand, we are expected to respond to Elsie's sentimental appeals for honesty and kindness, while Elsie, herself, is being dishonest for the sole purpose of helping her husband to more material success than he deserves.

IV *The Influence of Friends:*
The Deep Tangled Wildwood

Both *Dulcy* and *To the Ladies!* grew out of the association of
the playwrights with the Algonquin Round Table group, and
the evidence of that association is everywhere apparent in the
two plays. Adams' newspaper character had suggested the first
play, and the second play is a companion piece to the first. The
language of the two plays and the jokes were often directed to
the Round Table. In fact, in the second play there is a mention
of a character named "Benchley, an efficiency expert," a private
joke aimed at their mutual friend, Robert Benchley.

Connelly's life during these years, both personally and professionally, was centered around his New York friends; and it is
often difficult to tell what parts were personal and what parts
professional. In 1922, for example, the Vicious Circle of the
Hotel Algonquin produced a one-night show for some theater
friends. "The entertainment" was conceived when an actor complained that it was far easier for newspaper critics like Woollcott,
Kaufman, and Broun to review a performance than give one. In
answer, the Vicious Circle put together a variety show entitled
No Sirree!, which was shown Sunday evening, April 30, 1922.

Connelly was one of the most active members of the group in
the project. He sang in a chorus with Woollcott, Benchley, Kaufman, and Adams; and he played a variety of roles, including
"Mabel Cenci" in a skit, *The Editor Regrets;* the "Third Agi-
tated Seaman" in *The Greasy Hag,* a burlesque of an O'Neill
play; and "First Nighter" in a skit, *Between the Acts.* Also, he
gave "recitations with gestures, two of the favorites being 'You
Ask Me About the Crimea' and ... 'Barbara Frietchie'," and he
and Kaufman sang a song, "Kaufman and Connelly from the
West."[19] Laurette Taylor, the actress who reviewed the show
for the New York *Times,* May 1, 1922, advised Mr. Connelly
that he needed a course in voice culture. She was a little annoyed at the burlesque of O'Neill, but she concluded that Connelly and Kaufman were "the two who came out of it the best
. . . ."[20]

While Connelly and Kaufman were frolicking with the Vicious
Circle on stage, they were also getting their third play, *West of
Pittsburgh,* ready for production. It opened in May, and Frank-

lin P. Adams praised it in his column, May 30, 1922: "... saw the new play, 'West of Pittsburgh,' which points some sharp merriment at town-boosting and other pretenses...."[21] The play did not succeed, however; and revisions were made. Over a year later, on November 5, 1923, now given a new title, *The Deep Tangled Wildwood,* it opened at the Frazee Theatre in New York and ran for only sixteen performances. It was given poor reviews by all the newspaper critics, even by those who were friends of the playwrights.

Heywood Broun complained that "Very little creative imagination has gone into the plot." J. Rankin Towse called the play "a burlesque of a pretty thin, obvious, and ancient sort." Woollcott liked the "bright, fresh quips," but he considered the play a "somewhat commonplace fabric."[22] Even Adams, who praised the play as *West of Pittsburgh,* now reversed his opinion: "... 'The Deep Tangled Wildwood' [is] a comedy which began with great satirikall hilarity but oozed away, save for a few comic lines, to very little."[23]

The Deep Tangled Wildwood has never been published, and the only extant copy is the copyright manuscript in the Library of Congress. The playwrights, when the play was copyrighted, were still experimenting with the title, with four choices listed: *Little Old Millersville,* the title by which it was copyrighted and first known; *West of Pittsburgh,* the title by which it was first produced; and *Turn to the Left* and *Freedom of the City,* titles that appear nowhere else. There were probably some changes between this version and the one finally produced as *The Deep Tangled Wildwood,* but Mr. Connelly told me that such changes were largely stylistic. The main form of the play remained the same.

The play, in the version in the copyright manuscript, has a prologue and three acts that trace the attempts by a New York playwright, James Parks Leland, to "rediscover" himself by a return to his hometown, Millersville—a town that has much in common with Connelly's hometown, McKeesport. The prologue shows Leland in his New York apartment, following the failure of a new play, a play that even his friend, Harvey Wallick, admits was "very bad." Wallick, who is also his agent, is not worried: "You just had a nice rotten play in your system, and you got it out." Although he tells Leland that his last novel was "a

bit cheesy, too," he does not agree that a trip to Millersville will
be of any value.

It is not only the literary failures, however, but the New York
scene that depresses Leland: "The fads, the theatre! Theatre!
There's one trouble with me—I've got so close to the theatre that
I've been writing theatre instead of life." Back in Millersville, he
is certain, ". . . there is life, instead of delirium." His Aunt Sarah
Parks, moreover, has written him that she needs help, and Mary
Ellen, "the girl back home," has grown up.

But, when Leland arrives in Millersville, he finds changes have
taken place. During the war, the dye works—the town's only industry—has made everyone prosperous and foolish. The first act
is a parade of the pretensions of the townsfolk: the hired man
now runs a motion-picture theater; the seamstress owns a dress
"shoppe"; and the Ford agent is now the Buick distributor.
Everyone is in debt, and Leland is asked to help them get a new
loan. He is dismayed by the changes. Even Mary Ellen has become sophisticated. Only Deacon Flood, the old banker, and
Phyllis Westley, a young director from New York, seem "genuine"
to him. The first act ends with Leland's resolve to "save the
town" from itself.

The second act is built around a rehearsal of *The Warrior of
the Dawn,* a pageant the town is producing to celebrate its
growth. Most of this act is a broad burlesque of small-town
dramatics. Phyllis Westley, brought to Millersville to direct the
pageant, is intended to represent honest critical judgment; and
she demonstrates her honesty by telling Leland that his last novel
was a failure. At the same time, however, she seems to be unaware that the pageant is so bad that it is almost funny. She does
offer to resign as director, but this offer is prompted not by artistic considerations, but by a personal quarrel she has with the
star and backer of the show. In the midst of the dress rehearsal,
the town learns that it is "broke"; and then Leland tells the
people that he is responsible for their loan being refused. Fleeing
the town after his announcement, he takes a trip around the
world, leaving Millersville to find its soul during his absence.

The last act takes place a year later. Leland returns to find the
old Millersville. The modern taxis are gone, replaced by a horse
and buggy; and the "surplus" population—some seventy or eighty
thousand people who had been creating slums—has gone back to

wherever it came from. The people have become purified by the experience, and even thank Leland for saving them. As the play ends, however, a new source of wealth is discovered; and the town is ready to start on the "road to progress" once more. Leland, taking Phyllis with him, again flees to Europe, this time for a honeymoon, after which he and Phyllis will live in New York.

Here and there, as Woollcott commented,[24] there are some good touches, some interesting devices; and these Connelly used again in later works. Whatever the cause of the failure, however, one thing is certain: there is a basic split in the view of life. On the one hand, the play suggests an honest desire for the "simple life," a desire that Connelly developed more skillfully in later plays like *The Farmer Takes a Wife.* On the other hand, however, there is an implicit faith in modern civilization. Leland, even though he laments the changes in Millersville, knows the value of the complex society. He flees East, not West; and he settles again in New York, not in a small town.

V Merton of the Movies

Mr. Connelly says that the fault with *The Deep Tangled Wildwood* was that it lacked direction, he and Kaufman having listened to too many opinions in writing it. Fortunately for them, however, by the time it failed, they could, like Leland, afford a bad play. Between the time that *The Deep Tangled Wildwood* had its first production as *West of Pittsburgh* in May, 1922, and its Broadway opening in November, 1923, Connelly and Kaufman wrote *Merton of the Movies,* a play that is still probably the best comedy about the silent-film era of Hollywood that has ever been staged. If the failure of *The Deep Tangled Wildwood* points to the dangers of heeding the advice of literary friends, *Merton of the Movies* is an illustration of the advantages; for it was even more a result of the association with the Algonquin wits than were *Dulcy* or *To the Ladies!*.

On February 3, 1922, Franklin P. Adams reported to his newspaper readers that he had just read *Merton of the Movies* by Harry Leon Wilson and thought it an excellent story.[25] On the following day, Adams reported that he had spent the day with Connelly in a dime museum (a scene Connelly used later in *The Wild Man of Borneo*), "and saw the half-man and the sword swallower" and then went to see *To the Ladies!*, which was playing in New York.

Adams, from the beginning, was one of the most vocal supporters Kaufman and Connelly had; in fact, he was accused of "logrolling" on their behalf. It seems likely, therefore, that he at least mentioned Wilson's story to Connelly. It was George C. Tyler, the producer, however, who suggested that Connelly and Kaufman dramatize *Merton;* and, by the summer of 1922, *Merton of the Movies* was written as a play. Obviously, when it opened at the Cort Theatre in New York, on November 13, 1922, a great many people besides Connelly and Kaufman must have felt they had a share in its composition.

Harry Leon Wilson must have been pleased with the dramatization of his story, for in all the ways in which a work and its source may be examined mechanically, the stage *Merton* is faithful to the novel. The central action is about the same; even much of the dialogue is selected from the novel; and the characters in the play have their origins in Wilson's story. The play, however, has qualities not found in Wilson's story. The necessary economy of drama, as contrasted with the sprawling quality of the novel, is probably responsible for some of the difference; but the play, also, has a different tone. Connelly and Kaufman's *Merton of the Movies* is a laughing, tolerant analysis of the motion picture as an art form, whereas Wilson's novel is a satiric disapproval of the "hokum" of the movies in particular and the lack of culture in all American life in general. The characters in the play—Merton and the Montague Girl, especially—are, as a result, more sympathetic and more attractive than their counterparts in the novel. In the final analysis, Kaufman and Connelly carved out of Wilson's novel a better work of art, a more unified one, than the one they had found.

Merton of the Movies was a success from the first, both commercially and with the critics. John Gassner, for example, cited the play for its attack on the "vulgarization of art...."[26] Edmond Gagey called it "the best of the early satires" on Hollywood.[27] Joseph Wood Krutch saw in the play "the determination" of Kaufman and Connelly "to satirize those typical American institutions which the plain man was inclined to regard with reverence."[28] From the lack of attention paid to the play as drama, however, we would have to conclude that much of the critical respect for the play reflects more a feeling of distaste with the "movies" than pleasure with *Merton*.

Rather than satirizing the "vulgarization of the arts," it seems to me, *Merton of the Movies* suggests that one .should come to terms with the vulgar. Merton does win fame and fortune in the movies; and, as the curtain falls, he is telling a reporter for *Silver Screenings* the same kind of nonsense about himself that he once believed of others when he read the same magazine. This conclusion suggests that Merton has learned cynicism, a cynicism that will make it possible for him to succeed in the way of the world.

In part, all of Connelly and Kaufman's plays in this period contain caustic comments on the popularity of the cheap in art over the precious. In *Beggar on Horseback,* for example, the taste of the characters for "jazz" rather than for "high brow music" is made to demonstrate their shallow natures. In *Dulcy,* Leach's patronizing statements about Shakespeare are used to show his superficiality. "Yes, we're going to do some of Shakespeare's things next," Leach tells his audience, as he explains how the plays can be made to fit the silent films. "I was telling my director yesterday—I said, you know, Shakespeare had a tremendous feeling for plot. Of course, the dialogue is stilted for modern audiences—but then you don't have to listen to that in the pictures. He's still the master." In context, however, what is being attacked is not popular art forms as such—Kaufman and Connelly's own *Helen of Troy, N. Y.*[29] and *Be Yourself* are, after all, musical comedies, not operas—but the pretensions that argue the superiority of popular taste merely because it is financially profitable.

Merton of the Movies, in four acts and six scenes, shows the accidental rise of Merton Gill from a clerk in Gashwiler's General Store in Simsbury, Illinois, to a successful comic actor in a Jeff Baird parody. Merton's taste in motion pictures, it is true, is demonstrated to be debased. Back of his desires for Hollywood stardom is a "romantic passion" for Beulah Baxter, the "wonder woman of the silver screen," whom he has seen in a weekly serial, *Hazards of Hortense,* a parody of the *Perils of Pauline*—a popular Hollywood serial of the early 1920's.

Merton hopes that he can successfully imitate his hero, Harold Parmalee, and eventually co-star with Beulah Baxter. He is offended that the local movie theater runs Jeff Baird comedies on the same program with *Hazards of Hortense*. "Here's a wonderful artist [Beulah Baxter], trying to do better and finer things all the time, like *Hazards of Hortense*, and alongside of her they put a cheap thing like one of these Jeff Baird comedies." Merton is so offended at the Jeff Baird comedian, "the cross-eyed man," that he proclaims, "They oughtn't to allow them [Baird's comedies] to be made."

In Hollywood, Merton is slowly and painfully disabused of his notions of "the finer and better things" of the movies. Beulah Baxter is not only married, for the fourth time, to a crude fellow, but she is artistically dishonest. Although she had told Merton, through *Silver Screenings*, that to use a double for dangerous stunts was to break faith with "one's public," she herself uses one, the Montague Girl. While his "education" into the nature of Hollywood is taking place, Merton is tricked into playing a melodramatic part in a comedy. He thinks he is doing a "serious play," but the director is capitalizing on his unconscious burlesque of his hero, Harold Parmalee, and is using it as a parody. The movie is an immediate success, and Merton is a "star," even funnier than his "co-star" in the movie, "the cross-eyed man."

There is a moment of doubt concerning the success of the education, but Merton borrows a speech made about him and suggests that he was not fooled at all. "Don't you suppose I know as well as anybody that I've got a low-comedy face and that I couldn't make the grade in a serious picture?" he asks the heroine, the Montague Girl, who has "educated" him. And then he answers: "Straight satire—that's what I'm doing—and it's over the heads of most of my public. Why, they tell me that I was funnier than that cross-eyed man ever was in his life."

If satire is an imitation of the second-rate in art, all these plays can point to episodes—the *Sin* scene in *Dulcy*, the banquet scene in *To the Ladies!*—to demonstrate that Kaufman and Connelly are satirists. Such a concept of satire, more recently called *camp*, has been used to defend such modern burlesque as the *Batman* series on television. If satire is not merely an imitation of the bad, but a criticism that suggests a basis of what is good, however, these plays possess little.

Merton of the Movies, it is true, does suggest that in the short comedies—those then being made by Ben Turpin, "the cross-eyed man"; by Charlie Chaplin; and by Laurel and Hardy—Hollywood was doing its best work. It is suggested, moreover, that the comedy is superior to the "serious motion picture" in that it is honest in its aims and gets an honest response from the audience, laughter; but beyond that comment, the play has little to say about either Hollywood or American taste. Furthermore, in assessing *Merton of the Movies* as criticism of Hollywood, it should be noted that even before Wilson's story was published, "Mack Sennett, with the help of Ben Turpin's divinely crossed eyes, had consummated a burlesque of Messrs. Griffith, Inc. and Lubitsch, in *A Small Town Idol,* far more destructively, be it said, than Chaplin in his *Carmen,* and with faster fun than *Merton,*" at least according to Gilbert Seldes.[30]

If *Merton of the Movies* is not a serious attack on Hollywood—and seemingly Hollywood never thought it was, for it quickly turned the stage play into a screen play—it is, nevertheless, not meaningless drama. The play suggests an attitude toward life that is consistent with Mr. Connelly's lifelong philosophy. Merton, it is suggested, has come to some understanding of himself and life; and this understanding has made him tolerant not only of the faults of others, but of his own limitations.

The play was, in other respects, an advance in both theme and structure for the playwrights. They had not only given more thought to what they were saying in the play, but made far more imaginative use of the stage to say it. *Dulcy* was written for the conventional one-set, picture-frame stage; *To the Ladies!* merely showed that they had learned that the stage could accommodate more than one setting. *Merton of the Movies* demonstrated that the playwrights could conceive of the stage from an entirely different point of view, that of the *moving* camera. The action moves from scene to scene as though the sets were being filmed, an advance in staging that has gone but little noticed, largely, we assume, because the technique seems so natural to the subject.

VI The Forty-Niners and Other Frolics

During the 1922–23 season, while *Merton of the Movies* was proving a commercial success and *The Deep Tangled Wildwood* was resisting improvements by revision, Connelly joined the Vicious Circle for a second "entertainment"—this one titled *The Forty-Niners*. This show did not, however, repeat the success of *No Sirree!* In fact, Alexander Woollcott, who had performed in the first show, did not even like this one. He commented that "an evening's entertainment" with the "most gifted and most fantastic humorists" of the time—Connelly, Kaufman, Ring Lardner, F. P. Adams, and Dorothy Parker, among others—should have been, at least, enjoyable. "It wasn't fun," Woollcott concluded a review of it. "Not at all."[31]

During the winter of 1922–23, however, the two playwrights started on a musical comedy, *Helen of Troy, N. Y.*, which opened in June, 1923, for a successful run. The success of this musical must have offered some special satisfaction to the two men, both of whom had failed with musicals before joining forces. Connelly, especially, had been angry about the treatment given his first musical, *The Amber Princess*.

For some reason, in spite of its success on stage, *Helen of Troy, N. Y.* was never published; and the only extant copy of the book of the musical is the copyright manuscript. The story deals with a young secretary who works for a shirt factory in Troy, New York, and her adventures in getting the man she loves and saving the business for him. It is difficult to judge a musical comedy without its music, without its settings, without the embellishments that give it life; but a superficial reading of the book for this one leads to the conclusion that it was as meaningful and as amusing for its 1923 audience as *How to Succeed in Business Without Really Trying*, which has a book something like it, has been for more recent audiences.

VII   Beggar on Horseback

Helen of Troy, N. Y. had just opened when Kaufman and Connelly started on *Beggar on Horseback*, which is critically the most successful of all their collaborations. *Beggar on Horseback* opened in Wilmington, Delaware, on January 25, 1924; and within three weeks, on February 12, it was playing at the Broadhurst Theatre in New York, with Roland Young in the lead. This play was not so successful in its first run as *Dulcy, To the Ladies!, Merton of the Movies*, or the musical, *Helen of Troy*,

N. Y.; but it is the play, then and now, that has received the most serious critical attention, even from those who did not like it.

Professor Quinn, for example, concluded his study of the two playwrights with the judgment that in *Beggar on Horseback,* "The capacity of the co-authors for satire was revealed...."[32] Kenneth Macgowan did not like the play, but he found it an artistic improvement over their earlier works. Calling the authors, "the brightest beacons of The Conning Tower of F. P. A. and raconteurs of the self-named Vicious Circle of the Hotel Algonquin," Macgowan admitted that they had "pushed their satiric efforts past the conventional mixture of old-fashioned . . . skits," with which they had won early success.

> This is a dream play [Macgowan wrote] in which the composer-hero wanders through visions of the awful life which a marriage for money will entail. In a perfect forest of marble columns he is pursued by butlers that multiply in number. . . . And so *ad infinitum*—far too *infinitum*—until we have a sort of super-revue of the Cohan-cum-Intellectual variety with the music left out. The result is a sort of *Roger Bloomer* of the Algonquin. No beauty, of course, no stress; a reading from The Conning Tower instead of *The Dial.* Good satire, but, despite popular success, little that is essentially theatrical, no living and dynamic pattern....[33]

Another complaint against the work that was made often was that, like *Merton of the Movies, Beggar on Horseback* was an adaptation. Woollcott in a "Preface" to the first published edition of the play answered that criticism. He acknowledged that the play was "a derivative of Paul Apel's 'Hans Sonnenstoesser's Hohlenfahrt,' a short play produced in Germany some ten or twelve years ago," but beyond the idea of the play, he argued, Connelly and Kaufman owed little to Apel's work. Winthrop Ames, a producer, "had bought Apel's idea and when he turned his two young neighbors [Connelly and Kaufman] loose on that idea, all they obtained from the German original was such a notion of its general scheme as Ames might have imparted to them in a ten-minute conversation across the managerial desk."[34] All the best scenes in *Beggar on Horseback,* Woollcott concluded, "have no counterpart in the play Apel wrote."[35]

Whatever the individual critic may judge about the relative merits of plays that use other literary materials for suggestions, there should be little disagreement that in *Beggar on Horseback,* Connelly and Kaufman came to their fullest realization of the stage as a moving instrument for showing a point of view. John Gassner, in fact, lists this play as the first American drama to make successful use of Expressionism on the commercial stage.[36]

Beggar on Horseback, a play in two parts, has two kinds of action—one Realistic and one a dream. The Realistic action takes place in the hero's apartment and is conventional drawing-room comedy, much like *Dulcy.* Neil McRae, a young, talented musician, is working himself into a breakdown. He wants to write "serious" music, but, in order to support himself, he is forced to write orchestrations for "a cheap little music publisher." The girl-next-door, Cynthia, thinks such work is artistically degrading, "like copying bad prints"; moreover, the work leaves him no time or energy for his serious work. His friend, Dr. Albert Rice, advises him to marry wealth, a young piano student, Gladys Cady; and Cynthia, although she loves Neil, agrees with Dr. Rice.

Neil proposes to Gladys and is accepted; but then in a long dream—the Expressionistic part of the play—he discovers the evils of a marriage for money. When he awakens from his dream, he breaks his engagement to Gladys and proposes to Cynthia. As Gassner comments, the playwrights hardly deserve credit for "making so obvious a point," but they do deserve credit for the way in which they make it.[37]

In one respect, the earlier plays depended upon the very art forms they were ridiculing—the silent movies, the banquet speeches, the movie magazines—for their existence. In *Beggar on Horseback,* Connelly and Kaufman suggest what is worth having in art as well as what is worth avoiding. The Expressionistic scenes show the course of Neil's dream from the engagement, through the dream marriage and his introduction into business, to his trial for the mass murder of his dream wife and in-laws. Earlier the playwrights would probably have borrowed chunks of action from such events in life, paring them a little for dramatic economy, and inserted them into the play. The accounts of the movies in *Dulcy* and *Merton of the Movies,* for example, are merely thinly disguised accounts of then-current motion pictures, and not even the worst of these.

In the Realistic sections of *Beggar on Horseback,* the crassness of the get-rich-quick Cadys is shown as it existed among the get-rich-quick Americans of the early 1920's; but in the Expressionistic sections, life among the new-rich is also *interpreted*—not by the playwrights' spokesman in the guise of a character—but by an artistic distortion of real events that shows the value, or lack of it, of such a life. The Cadys, in the Realistic section, for example, *talk* of their butlers; but in the Expressionistic section, the butlers multiply for each occasion, demonstrating *dramatically* that they are symbols of success that tyrannize the society. In the Realistic scenes, the interferences of the outside world that keep Neil from his work are shown—Gladys' interruptions and the blare of the music from a café next door; but in the Expressionistic scenes they are made into a ceremony of torture.

Throughout the play, the music of Deems Taylor, who for a time shared an apartment with Connelly, is heard; and a central scene of Part Two is the performance of Taylor's pantomime, "A Kiss in Xanadu," which Adams told his readers was "the only pantomime that did not bore me."[38] This scene and the uses made of it in the Expressionistic part of *Beggar on Horseback* demonstrate that in this play Kaufman and Connelly were willing to show their commitment to an art that is imaginative and difficult, that searches for depth.

To go from *Beggar on Horseback* to the contemporary dramas of the absurd is to suggest a cause-effect relationship that does not really exist. It is significant, however, that, although Connelly can never accept the rejection of the world found in so much of the drama of the absurd, he yet has considerable admiration for the talents of Albee, Ionesco, Beckett, and Giraudoux.[39] The absurdists did not, it seems safe to assume, go to *Beggar on Horseback* for their theatrical devices, but they could find many of them there. The gathering of the business leaders in *Beggar on Horseback,* for example, has much in common with the opening café scene in Jean Giraudoux's *The Mad Woman of Chaillot;* the expressionistic Mrs. Cady, with her attached rocking chair, has an affinity with the characters in Edward Albee's *Sandbox;* the peopling of the stage with imaginary characters anticipates Eugene Ionesco's *The Chairs.*

Such parallels are not cited to suggest that the theater of the absurd starts with *Beggar on Horseback;* Kaufman and Connelly borrowed many of these devices from earlier Continental drama. The play, however, is a considerable advance in the use of imaginative techniques for a freer stage; and, in the context of the popular Broadway plays of the 1920's, this advance amounts almost to a revolution.

Kenneth Macgowan's complaint against the play—that it is "a sort of super-revue of the Cohan-cum-Intellectual variety"—is, unfortunately, in part valid. There are, perhaps, too many devices, any one of which, as *The Chairs* demonstrates, could serve as the controlling metaphor for the entire play. His summary judgment, "And so *ad infinitum,*" is not a complaint against the variety and number of the devices, but an objection to the tone that results.

In spite of the courage of Connelly and Kaufman, in bringing to the popular stage a kind of drama then only defended in the *avant garde* theater, they almost apologize for their daring in the Realistic parts of the play. The audience is made aware from the beginning that the Expressionism is a man's dream; and, since Neil is near a nervous breakdown, it is also suggested that the dream is distorted. Neil in his restful dreams would never commit murder, never be so disdainful of money and the time it buys. Neil comes to no understanding of life in his dream that a five-minutes' conversation with a rich woman's husband would not have given him, and we may suspect that Cynthia's nagging encouragement of Neil's genius will eventually prove as disastrous as Gladys' silliness.

Even with reservations, however, most readers would agree with Joseph Mersand that, in its time, *Beggar on Horseback* "was breaking new ground in the American theatre by its courageous attack on the crushing effects of big-business mentality upon artistic creation."[40] If Connelly's career had ended with this play, we would have to lament that he stopped writing at the moment of his greatest promise. As Professor Quinn concluded in assessing Connelly's contribution to his collaborations with Kaufman, Connelly brought to the drama "the imaginative quality that lifted *Beggar on Horseback* into permanent value."[41] Undoubtedly, Connelly needed the sense of form that Kaufman contributed; but *Beggar on Horseback* suggests that Connelly's particular talent needed a freer rein than Kaufman's sense of "compact structure" would permit before he would be able to write *The Green Pastures*.

VIII *The End of the Collaboration*

Beggar on Horseback was the most successful artistic collaboration that Connelly and Kaufman made; and, ironically, it was their last full-length, straight drama. In the fall following this play, on September 23, 1924, a second musical, *Be Yourself*, by Connelly and Kaufman opened at the Sam H. Harris Theatre in New York.[42] It was commercially successful, but neither man seemingly considered it much more than an exercise in talent. In fact, there is now apparently no copy of the play still extant.

It was probably during this time, too, that Connelly and Kaufman collaborated on a one-act play, *Service*. The play was not copyrighted until 1932 and seems never to have been produced or published, the only extant copy now being the copyright manuscript.[43] *Service* is a short parody of the theater-management service of the 1920's; and the barbs are aimed especially at the theater ticket brokers.

There was no quarrel between the two men. Each one simply felt that he had things to do that he needed to do alone. Mr. Connelly, in fact, and seemingly Mr. Kaufman, too, did not really plan for their separation to be permanent; and a number of times in the years that followed, they discussed writing another play together. Judging from the standards of success for the New York theater in the early 1920's, it would be difficult to find any goal that they had not achieved in their collaborations which they could reasonably have hoped to achieve singly. The academic and art-magazine critics, it is true, gave them little notice; and, perhaps, they would have liked some of the adulation that was then being given to O'Neill, who had started his playwriting at the same time.

On the other hand, however, as the burlesque they did of O'Neill in *No Sirree!* suggests, Kaufman and Connelly lived in a different world and knew it. They valued honesty, but for them an honest view of life had gaiety in it. They respected decency, but found they could achieve a decent life through wit, luck, and work—not through suffering. Problems of loneliness, rejection, and isolation they recognized; but their own such problems were solved by membership in one of the most congenial groups of wits ever gathered in New York. For those who know only the Romantic ideal of the suffering artist, they present another image—that of the American writer who is happy with his lot.

While it would be grossly unfair to conclude that Kaufman and Connelly were merely commercial writers, it is yet true that they were "professional writers." Writing for them was a cause, but it was first a job and an activity. They lived with a sense of the immediate that now makes some of their work seem dated, and often their point of view was limited in time and space to the Broadway scene of the mid-1920's. Only four of their plays— *Dulcy, To the Ladies!, Merton of the Movies,* and *Beggar on Horseback*—were ever published; but *Merton* and the *Beggar,* at least, are more than period pieces. Although they are focused upon scenes, which, in their obvious details, at least, have changed, they do offer, in forms that are still exciting, a view of life that is still valid.

CHAPTER 3

Years of Wisdom and Wit,
New Yorker Style

MARC CONNELLY has had a reputation throughout his life for being an easygoing sort of fellow. Alexander Woollcott, for example, was certain that, after the termination of the Connelly-Kaufman partnership, Connelly would never do any serious work. He was, in Woollcott's judgment, "an innocent,"[1] "a procrastinator and peacock."[2] Robert Benchley, who had a much better understanding of Connelly, had a different opinion. "Mr. Connelly," he wrote, "must write a perfect play or he will have none of it."[3]

There probably is not another major writer in all American literature who has the affection of so many of his fellow artists as Marc Connelly. He has always been a man of principle, generous and tolerant. He is, moreover, modest, probably to a fault, and excellent company. He has a spirit of adventure and is never bored; and, although he possesses many talents, it is almost impossible to be jealous of any of them, for Mr. Connelly has spent most of his life "exploring" his talents and little time "exploiting" any one of them.

During the five years from 1925 to 1930, for example, years that his biographers and critics now view as an almost inactive period, Connelly wrote two first-rate comedies, *The Wisdom Tooth* and *The Wild Man of Borneo;* one musical comedy, *How's the King?;* a series of one-act plays about a character named Kenneth Mercer; ten short stories; and one art drama, *Ex Cathedra,* for *Theatre Arts.* During these five years, too, he helped Harold Ross found *The New Yorker,* directed and acted in plays, and did the basic research for *The Green Pastures.*

Unfortunately for Connelly's reputation with academic scholars, only about half of this work has ever been published; and much of that half is no longer easily available. In 1930, after the success of *The Green Pastures* was assured, Walter Prichard Eaton wrote of Connelly's career: he "didn't exactly wake up one February morning" in 1930 and find himself famous; for, "In the first place, he probably hadn't been asleep, and in the second, he was famous already." For the years from the end of Connelly's collaborations with Kaufman until *The Green Pastures,* however, Eaton could find only two works that added to Connelly's "stature as a dramatist, and the measure of his fame"—" 'The Wisdom Tooth,' which had a moderate success, and ... [a play] with H. J. Mankiewicz, . . . 'The Wild Man of Borneo,' which was a failure."[4]

During these five years, however, Connelly, in addition to writing for the theater, did a considerable amount of work for *The New Yorker*—short stories, one-act plays, skits, essays, and various editorial chores. Such work was done, largely, because Connelly knew that Harold Ross, the editor, needed help with what was then an uncertain venture. Of all this work, four of the short stories—"Barmecide's Feast," "The Guest," "The Dear Old Couple," and "Happiest Man in the World"—and one play, *The Traveler,* have been anthologized. For the most part, the rest is available only in the original issues of *The New Yorker;* and, since it was not until after 1930 that the contents of that journal were indexed, the modern reader interested in Connelly's work published in it must go through each issue page-by-page; and copies of *The New Yorker* for the first years of its existence are rare.

It is perhaps understandable, then, that Mr. Connelly has a reputation for indolence and procrastination; but a review of his work for this period suggests that a qualification needs to be made in the accusation. As a creative artist, Mr. Connelly was about as active during these years as in any other like period in his life. As an editor of his own works and as an exploiter of his own talents, he displayed an indifference to a reading public —or an unwillingness to create a reading audience for anything he felt was not "perfect."

A somewhat detailed review of Connelly's works of this period, both the published and unpublished ones, is thus the intention of this chapter. It should be noted that many of these works now exist only in the author's typed manuscripts in the Library of Congress, some of which are not in "polished" form. It is anticipated, however, that some of these works will be published in the next few years. Mr. Connelly, at the time this manuscript was being prepared, had made arrangements with the University of Wisconsin to give his manuscripts to its American drama collection.

I   The Wisdom Tooth

The Wisdom Tooth,[5] from the beginning, has received considerable praise. Quinn, calling it "a charming comedy," argued that "it seems to settle the question as to which member of the original partnership [Connelly or Kaufman] contributed the imaginative quality that lifts *To the Ladies!* and *Beggar on Horseback* into permanent value."[6] F. P. Adams saw it on opening night, February 24, 1926, and called it "very fine . . . and beautifully acted too. . . ."[7] Burns Mantle selected it as one of the "best plays" of the 1925-26 season, and Doran and Company published it.

The praise, to be sure, was qualified; but so also were the complaints. Stark Young, for example, complained about Connelly's lack of "social philosophy; his play has only implications of social satire, only little hints and implications at that." Young complained, too, about the lack of "universality" in the play. "His hero," he wrote, "is a single case and we are to watch his fortunes more, I gather, for the sentiment involved, the fantasy and the homely romance, than for any sting or theory about our society, our national or local characteristics, our blurred uniformity." It is, moreover, Young argues, only with the introduction of the fantasy that the play becomes interesting: "After this point it [the play] brightens up, strengthens its tone, and then subsides again gradually into what it was before, homely fantasy, comedy of sentiment, amusing and obvious accuracies of small observations."[8]

Fred B. Millet commented on the play in terms that show his basic agreement with Young's criticism. The play, he wrote, deals again, as *Beggar on Horseback* had, with "the deadening effect of business on the sensitive individual"; but, he concludes, "what one remembers [after the play] is the Barriesque juxtaposition of the corrupted adult and the fine boy he used to be."[9]

It is probably a mistake to assume that *The Wisdom Tooth* was intended to be social criticism. Little in Connelly's personal life during these years suggests that he felt any great dissatisfaction with his society and especially with the New York business world. He was concerned then, and is now, with the struggle of the separate individual to maintain his decency, his courage, and his sense of fantasy in any world of dull, opinionated fellows and mechanical routine. There is—as a later play, *Land of the Living*, suggests—a great deal more of Thoreau than of Sinclair Lewis[10] in Marc Connelly.

If *The Wisdom Tooth* is to be seen or read most rewardingly, we should, it seems to me, understand that the play is not concerned with the "trapped victim" of the industrial machine, nor with his "fortunes" as he tries to escape "the system." *The Wisdom Tooth*, rather, is concerned with individual wisdom, which is always a personal, private matter; and the play shows a man who feels that he is losing his sense of the personal adventure of life in the mechanical operation of "getting along."

Like *Beggar on Horseback*, this play opens with a conventionally Realistic scene, moves into an Expressionistic interlude, and then returns to the Realistic world made better—more "Romantic"—for the hero by the dream experience. Like the protagonist of *Beggar on Horseback*, Charley Bemis in *The Wisdom Tooth* learns enough from his dream to make a decent choice in the real world. *The Wisdom Tooth* is, however, better controlled than *Beggar on Horseback*. Professor Macgowan's complaint that *Beggar on Horseback* is "a sort of super-revue of the Cohan-cum-Intellectual variety" has never been suggested of *The Wisdom Tooth*. In fact, the most common criticism has been that *The Wisdom Tooth* needs more of the "super-revue" quality. Theatrically, we would probably agree with Young and Millet that the second act, which deals with Bemis' return to the world of his youth, is perhaps the most interesting; but any consideration of the play as a unified work of art would force us to the conclusion that Connelly in *The Wisdom Tooth* has achieved the proper balance between the Expressionistic devices and the Realistic form for *his* purposes.

If the critic discards the notion that Connelly's purpose *should be* social criticism, the obvious theme of the play is clear enough. Charley Bemis, a senior clerk, is introduced in the first scene in a depressingly Realistic setting, "A men's washroom." Bemis, a timid man, gives evidence of his basically decent nature. He would defend a young woman, the Duchess, who has been fired. His sense of fair play and chivalry is offended by the reasons which two of his fellow employees—Sparrow and Carter—give for her dismissal. "Maybe he [J. H. Porter, the president of the company] tried to get fresh with her." "The boss's wife couldn't stand her." Bemis, who is suffering from a toothache, thinks something should be done; but, when Porter enters the scene, Bemis is too timid to translate his desires into action. In the face of authority, he deserts his principles. "I did the sensible thing," he tells the others when they ridicule him for his failure to take a stand.

In the second scene of the first act, Bemis again loses a battle, this time between Realism and Fantasy—thus establishing the principle that courage and a belief in fantasy are somehow related. While waiting in the dentist's office, he admits to the other patients that his grandmother believed in fairies. "Maybe your grandmother was a little cuckoo," one patient tells him; and another warns, "Don't tell a cop you believe in things like that, or they'll put you in the funny house." Before the force of ridicule, Bemis flees without ever seeing the dentist.

The third scene of the first act completes the picture of the world of simple Realism in which Bemis lives. He has gone from the office, symbolized by the men's washroom, to the dentist's office; and in this scene he now comes to his home, a boarding house in the West Seventies. Here, in a political discussion with another boarder, Farraday, Bemis again proves himself a coward. Farraday, with "a few remarks, utterly without logic," makes Bemis agree that Coolidge is really a good President. Bemis is, Farraday tells Sally, the girl Bemis loves, a man with "No mind of his own—no point of view."

As the first act ends, Bemis' life has been depicted in its totality. He is—at home, in the world, and at the office—a man who has lost the courage of his convictions, his sense of fantasy, his belief in his private wisdom. He has, in his own terms, become a "carbon copy." At the end of the act, when the spirit of his dead grandmother comes to him, he tells her, "Gee! I certainly need your help."

The first scene of the second act, still in the boarding house, demonstrates Bemis' belief in the world of spirits, the world of fantasy, the world of his youth. The spirits of his grandparents and the fairy, Lalita, come alive to him and, in his dream, to the other boarders. Belief, however, is only half of Bemis' problem. When the other boarders (now characters in Bemis' dream world) object to his spirits, he lacks the courage to defend them. Grandpa, witnessing such cowardice, is certain that Bemis is not the man who was his grandson; and, as the scene ends, Bemis, at Sally's urging, goes back to his youth to find the boy he had been. "And when you find him," Sally tells him, "bring him back to me."

Bemis finds his youth, the boy-he-was, Skeeter, in a circus; but the differences between the man and the boy are emphasized, not reconciled, by the meeting. Skeeter believes in his spirits and is willing to fight to protect them, but Bemis again proves a coward, and Skeeter assumes the job of saving him. "We're going years and years away from here," he tells Grandpa at the end of the third scene of the second act. "This old thing [Bemis] and me are going on an adventure. ... We're going to J. H. Porter and Company, Incorporated, and avenge a woman's good name."

In the last scene of the second act, Bemis, with Skeeter's encouragement, faces Porter, finds he has been mistaken, and gains not only his own self-respect but Porter's approval and a promotion. His victory, of course, has been achieved only in the dream world, in his fantasy; and, in the third act, Bemis returns to the real world, the one of the aching tooth.

He now understands—and admits to himself—that he is a ridiculous man, a timid man with a cloth tied around his face for a toothache. But the dream that has brought him to this understanding also helps him to see that the "practical men" of this world—the office worker who borrows money to impress a young lady and the opinionated Farraday—are also ridiculous. He is now ready to face the real J. H. Porter.

"Don't be too rash about it, Charley," Sally tells him; but Bemis knows now that on matters of principle one often needs to be rash. In the real world, however, the reward for courage and principle is not promotion; Bemis is fired.

"Not that I blame him much, either," Bemis tells Sally "Or not that I care a damn." Tomorrow he will need to find new employment, but tonight he intends to learn a new game of cards from Sally. Whatever his problems in the material world may be, Bemis has recovered his sense of play.

What disturbed Stark Young about the play was the lack of social philosophy. Although the play suggests that most clerks live lives of quiet desperation, it is not really the system that is being condemned. Bemis will continue to earn his living in the future as he has in the past, and his next job and his next employer will probably be no better or no worse than his last ones. Bemis is not in revolt against society; he is in revolt against what he has allowed himself to become. Connelly's suggestion that self-esteem can be restored by the courage and imagination of youth may not be earth-shattering social philosophy, but it is a theme that is realized in all parts of the play. *The Wisdom Tooth*, because it limits itself to one theme, is a better unified play than *Beggar on Horseback;* and, as a work of art, if not as an editorial comment, it is the best work that Connelly had done up to that time.

II *Wild and Tame*

Unfortunately for Connelly, the start that he had made for an independent reputation as a playwright with *The Wisdom Tooth* was followed by *The Wild Man of Borneo*,[11] a wonderfully conceived play that started wrong and never recovered. Back in the days of Connelly's collaborations with Kaufman, the two playwrights had promised Herman J. Mankiewicz, Kaufman's assistant on the New York *Times,* that they would collaborate with him on a play. "Mank was a wonderfully entertaining companion," Mr. Connelly told me, "but he was a coffee-klatcher, who confused talk about what he wanted to do with work done."

When Mankiewicz came to Connelly with an outline for a sketch that he thought could be developed into a play, Connelly agreed; and it was not until sometime later that he realized that the sketch Mankiewicz had given him was one that he, Connelly, had written a few years earlier for W. C. Fields and Bea Lillie. Both men, however, were credited with joint authorship of *The Wild Man of Borneo* when it opened September 13, 1927, at the

Bij Theatre in New York;[12] and the play is now listed in the-
at histories by "Marc Connelly and Herman J. Mankiewicz."
t, according to Mr. Connelly, Mankiewicz did little more than
ead the finished script. The problem of determining authorship
has, however, never been a serious one. The play ran for only
fifteen performances and closed with generally unfavorable reviews. Connelly accepted the judgment of the reviewers. The
play was withdrawn, and has never been published or produced
again.

It is understandable that Connelly should be disappointed
with the reception, but we doubt that a contemporary playwright
would allow a play of like merit to be so quickly discarded.
Frank Hanley's *Slow Dance on the Killing Ground,* for example,
was unsuccessful at the box office and was withdrawn, but it has
since been published and is now helping to establish Hanley's
reputation with literary critics. In the 1920's, however, even
with a playwright with Connelly's reputation, there was more
readiness to drop any play that was not immediately successful
on the stage.

The reviews, as a matter of fact, were not altogether damning.
John Mason Brown was disappointed with parts of the play, but
he acknowledged that "This comedy ... comes ... tantalizingly
near to achieving its comic purpose," although he also complained about the "half-written Algonquins of its humor" and the
"old-fashioned plotting of a comedy of the eighties...."[13]
Stark Young liked the play. "We begin," he wrote, "in a boarding-house, kept adorably by Miss Josephine Hull, with that quality ... that runs between pathos and giggles. .... A new lodger
... J. Daniel Thompson ... arrives with his daughter.... His
past has been on the road with medicine shows. He pretends
that he is alternating with Richard Mansfield in Cyrano, but in
reality he is ... to play the Wild Man of Borneo [in a dime
"freak" museum].... His daughter, her lover, and the people
from the boarding-house find him at the museum. The story
ends with his daughter's marriage ... and their persuading Mr.
Thompson to go on with the wild man." Young blamed Connelly's staging and George Hassell's acting of the Thompson
role for the failure.[14]

Burns Mantle's summary of the play suggests that it failed because Connelly did not keep his purpose clear. *The Wild Man*

of Borneo, according to Mantle, is a play about Thompson's attempts "to make good" with his daughter "by telling her that he
is a great and prosperous actor when in reality he has never been
anything but a cheap medicine show faker."[15] Whatever it was
in the production that caused Mantle to interpret Thompson's
character in this manner, it is quite clear in the written script
that Thompson is much more than a "cheap medicine show faker." He is, in fact, a kind of American Cyrano; and, remembering
Connelly's introduction to theater with *Cyrano de Bergerac,*[16]
we should understand that, for him, Cyrano is a poet whose imagination saves the soul from the humdrum world of petty pretenses.

Young's summary is accurate enough in the main outlines.
Thompson does pretend to be playing Cyrano, while, in truth,
he is the Wild Man; he is exposed and does agree to keep the
role. The summary, however, lacks all appreciation of the careful motivation that is built into the role. Thompson likes the life
of the confidence man, not because he has fallen into it, but because he has risen to it. He is, as his daughter's lover says, the
king of con artists. In the third act, after he has been exposed,
Thompson receives a proposal of marriage from his landlady, a
former actress who, having toured as Lady Dracula in her youth,
can appreciate his artistry as the Wild Man of Borneo. He rejects
her offer, explaining that he is a "bum." She argues that he is a
poet, and he does not disagree. In fact, he makes it clear that
his pretenses are his means, not of victimizing others, but of stay-
ing free.

What makes it difficult to see Thompson as a Cyrano is both
the lack of poetic diction of the play and the absence of melodramatic villains. The real threat to individual freedom in society is not the conscious oppression of the free man by fools and
rogues. Such freedom is threatened rather by the conventional
habits of conventional people getting on in the world. These
people are innocent; but, except for rare moments when they
meet and sympathize with a man like Thompson, they lead lives
of dull routine.

There is little change in the character of Thompson in the
play, and change would be necessary if this were to be a conventional comedy about the reform of a confidence man. As the first
act ends, for example, Thompson, to please his daughter, dic-

tates a letter: "Dear President of Vassar College, kindly send me your latest catalogue together with lowest rates and references. I am thinking of sending my daughter. . . ." At the end of the play, he is telling a fantastic story of his adventures as the sole survivor of the Custer Massacre to please the young child, Francine. The critics, in the main, interpreted these speeches as Thompson's attempts to impress others, to be a faker; but the play itself makes it clear that his only motive is to please. Ed La-Motte, his daughter's lover, is the only one aware of Thompson's motives and character. He would, it should be noted, profit from Thompson's exposure; but he has great respect for him.

Although Thompson does not change himself—and it is suggested that any change would be a loss—he does change the people about him, and always for the better. Mrs. Diamond, an actress, discovers through his "lies" that she loves her husband and that he loves her, although the one certain fact of her existence before she met the Wild Man was that she hated her husband. Birdo, another entertainer, is a sour, suspicious man, half in love with Mrs. Marshall when the play opens. At the end of the play—although he has attempted to expose Thompson—he is a man with a new appreciation of his own talent for bird imitations and an admiration for Thompson's many talents; and his love affair with Mrs. Marshall has taken on meaning.

The theme of *The Wild Man of Borneo* is clear enough in the written script: life is essentially good, and people are decent; but sometimes it takes an imaginative "lie" to show the truth. Thompson's reading of lines from his Cyrano role and his performance as the Wild Man are both intended to demonstrate that he is a great actor, a poet with visions, a man of artistic courage. Like Cyrano, Thompson does not win a final battle, does not prove anything about society; but there is victory enough for Connelly in the survival of Thompson's "white plume," his poetic nature.

III   The Gay Deceiver

While *The Wild Man of Borneo* was still in rehearsal, Connelly was getting another new play ready. In 1927, John Mason Brown mentioned in a review of the coming season that this new play would be titled *The Gay Deceiver*.[17] This mention is the only one of such a play, and Mr. Connelly now has no recollections of that title. *The Gay Deceiver*, seemingly, was an earlier title for *How's the King?*, a musical that Connelly copyrighted in 1925. It was produced in 1927 by Earl Carroll, but the production was so shoddy that, even after forty years, Connelly still feels some resentment: "... some of the scenery fell down on opening night." Mr. Connelly, in fact, now has only a fragmentary copy of the play in his possession; and his copyright manuscript, on file in the Library of Congress,[18] although not entirely complete, appears to be the only extant copy.

How's the King? should more properly be called a farce with variety-show routines than a musical comedy, for the various parts of the show are only weakly integrated into the central action. It is, in some respects, a series of skits—with the same kind of basic jokes and dialogue that Connelly used later in his Mr. Mercer one-act plays. The central action of the play deals with King Theodore Carl the Third and his attempts to sell his kingship to various rich Americans—Joe, the hero of the play; Senator Alexander, who wants a kingdom to please his wife; and Jones and Beatty, who buy the title and the kingdom as a real estate venture.

In the lengthy "Prologue," Joe explains how he happened to buy his kingship, while Kenneth Firestone, his Italian barber and minister of affairs, plays the guitar for background music:

> Well, sir, or well, madam, [Joe explains] ... It's like this; about four months ago I was seated in my great lonely mansion ... and in walks a fellow with ... a lot of Titians and Rembrandts and a couple of Raphaels and a very good early Harrison Fisher. He said he's heard that I was a rich millionaire of great wealth and wanted I should lend him a million dollars, in exchange for the old masters. . . . . Well, he almost had me, when I remembered a friend of mine loaned a fellow money like that once ... and then the fellow sued him. So, I says, "No." Then the fellow says, "Well, how would you like to buy a throne?"

The "fellow" is the legitimate King of Uric, and he makes the same offer to other "kings." His intention is to sell his kingdom for two million dollars each to three victims and then to abscond to New York and open a nightclub.

The two acts of the play deal with Joe's romance with Jerry

Langdon, a New York girl, who met and "half-married" the legitimate King one night in Paris. Joe's problem is to keep the marriage from being completed; and, with the help of a mule, Park Avenue, he succeeds. The play moves from one "routine" to another; and the routines are controlled by the device of presenting the musical as a play in progress. In the "Prologue," the audience is reminded that *How's the King?* is only a play. When Joe completes an address to "his people," he concludes, "And, if, in my poor efforts, I have been able to make one of you smile and forget his troubles for a brief hour, then the author will feel that this little book has not been written in vain."

Connelly's purpose for this musical was obviously only that— to make the audience forget its "troubles for a brief hour." The play has no real satiric purpose, although it scatters "irreverent" comments on all kinds of social institutions. The King is not a villain, but rather "The Gay Deceiver," less a swindler than a happy clown. This play is easier to review favorably than to analyze profitably, a more inventive work than *Helen of Troy, N.Y.;* but—at least in the only extant script—it is not so carefully plotted.

IV   *The Mercer Plays*

Some of Connelly's plays that deserve far more attention than they have received are his Kenneth Mercer skits. From 1925 through the early 1930's, Connelly wrote and produced several of them, but allowed just one to be published. In 1939, the Dramatists Play Service published *The Traveler* for stage production;[19] and it is now the only play of the group that is listed among Connelly's acting plays. The other plays in this group —*The Bridegroom,*[20] *The Burglar,*[21] *The Suitor,*[22] and *The Uncle*[23]—are of equal merit; and all of the plays have a special interest for anyone concerned with Connelly the man, for they are—in part—plays in which Connelly has used himself as the real-life model for his comic protagonist, Kenneth Mercer.

The central episode of *The Traveler* has to do with a man, Kenneth Mercer, who rides a transcontinental train for one city stop in New York, a matter of a few miles. The basic "plot" was one that Connelly had used earlier in one of his oral "droll stories," but the point of the oral story was that Mercer was as worried as if he were making a long trip. In the play, however, Connelly sacrifices the joke and makes the trip an "extraordinary one" for the man.

In an age when trains still suggested the romance of travel, *The Traveler* must have been wonderfully funny; and indeed, even now, the wit and charm shine through what has become—because of the success of such pieces as this—a kind of museum piece. The play, set in the smoking compartment of a Pullman car, opens in darkness with the voice of the train master announcing the names of far-off places: "Bo-a-rd! Twentieth Century Limited for Albany, Utica, Syracuse, Buffalo, Cleveland, and Chicago. First stop—One Hundred and Twenty-fifth Street." The first stop is the destination for Kenneth Mercer, but the audience is not immediately aware of this fact as Morton, the porter, ushers in Mr. Mercer, "holding several bundles, with an overcoat over his arm." At first, the play seems to be a satire—a good-natured, light satire—about a man on his first transcontinental train ride. Mercer is nervous and grateful for advice on comfortable travelling. He is sentimental about leaving familiar surroundings: "Good-by, old Grand Central Station!"

In his interview with the patient conductor, Mr. Barclay, Mercer reveals, however, that he is a man who has made an heroic effort to change his routine, to do something different, and Connelly sympathizes with his effort and has admiration for his courage and good will. Mercer realizes he is in a new world and anxiously hopes to relate his new experience to his past life. He asks, "Do you ever get around to my stamping ground, Mr. Barclay?"

BARCLAY. Which stamping ground *is* that, Mr. Mercer?
MERCER. One Hundred and Twenty-fifth Street.
BARCLAY. Not very often....
MERCER. I just thought you might know some people in my neck of the woods.

Mercer and Barclay finally do discover a common bond. The conductor has read the advertisements for Mastbaum and Sons Furniture, and Mercer tells him: "I guess I've gone past Mastbaum's store a couple of hundred times." The bond, however slim, is enough to please Mr. Mercer.

The play has no melodramatic action. Mercer boards the train at Grand Central Station; talks for a few minutes with the porter and a few with the conductor, all on matters of the most trivial nature; arrives at his stop; and leaves the train. Mr. Connelly, however, charges the scene with nervous tension, making the audience see in Mercer a representative of all routine men. Playwrights of the 1960's would have made Mercer's anxiety explode into an act of violence, a rejection of the "professional" kindness of the conductor, as Edward Albee, for example, does in *The Zoo Story.* Connelly's anxious man, however, is merely grateful for polite concern, so grateful in fact that he is now ready to repeat the adventure. "I'll tell you what!" Mercer tells Barclay as he departs, "We'll do the whole trip over again this summer."

The Traveler was the first of the Kenneth Mercer plays; and, although this character varies in age and certain visible characteristics from one play to the next, Mercer always has a relationship to his creator, Marc Connelly. During these years, Connelly was a successful playwright, a bachelor-about-town in his mid-thirties. In 1930, at the age of thirty-nine, he surprised his friends by marrying the Hollywood actress, Madeline Hurlock. In the second of these plays, *The Bridegroom,* a play filmed by RKO–Radio Pictures, but never published, Connelly, in the role of Mercer, pokes fun at his own real-life role of romantic suitor.

The scene for *The Bridegroom* is Mercer's bedroom, the morning of his wedding to the beautiful Genevieve. Mercer, who has attended a bachelor party that did not end until three-thirty that morning, is much in need of help; and it is supplied by his friend, Harvey. With but "six minutes" left before the wedding ceremony is to begin, Mercer has forgotten to put on his trousers; and his dress shirt is covered with the signatures of his bachelor-dinner guests. He dimly remembers the party and is filled with remorse for his behavior. Through the ache of a hangover, he is certain that he is not "good enough" for Genevieve. Although Harvey tells him that Genevieve loves him, Mercer has his doubts about the success of the marriage. "I know," he says, "but whoever heard of a fellow without any hair getting a beautiful girl like that?" Connelly then leaps from a personal joke that his friends had shared for ten years, from 1920 when he started to lose his hair, to the comedy of the illogical: "What if we have children and they're bald-headed? I haven't been able to sleep thinking of it," he tells Harvey. "Little children should not suffer."

The arrival of the bride's father, Mr. Montgomery, telling him to hurry, prevents any last-minute change of plans; but Mercer is worried about the ring. He tries it on; and, since it will not fit him, he is certain he has the wrong ring until Harvey reminds him that the ring is for Genevieve. Resigned to his joy, if not confident, Mercer starts for the altar; but the last battle has not yet been won:

> "Oh," he gasps.
> "What is it now?" Harvey asks in exasperation.
> "What's her name?"
> "Genevieve."

And, as the curtain falls, Mercer moves to his fate, muttering, "Genevieve. . . ."

In another skit, *The Burglar,* Mercer is the comfortable, well-to-do bachelor. This play takes place on an evening when he stumbles upon a burglar in the process of robbing his apartment. When the burglar greets him with, "Well, Mr. Inquisitive, what do you want?" Mercer is certain he must be a friend or relative. He attempts to guess, "Harry Ferdecker? .... Reverend Bernard Rapley? .... Not Aunt Elizabeth on one of her...?" The burglar, Mr. McQuebb, finally removes his mask to assure Mercer that they are not acquainted; but Mercer refuses to be convinced that McQuebb is a genuine burglar. McQuebb shows him his card, "McQuebb and Crouse. General Burglary." Crouse, it seems, is "temporarily retired"; but, if Russel Crouse—in one of whose plays Connelly was later to play a leading role—missed Connelly's reference, the association of burglary and theater is emphasized by McQuebb's actor-like concern with his press notices: "Rhode Island Red McQuebb gets 12 years for stealing old telephone books," which, McQuebb informs Mercer, is the "record sentence for that particular kind of crime."

Mercer is impressed and tries to be useful to McQuebb, who is merely annoyed by advice from an amateur. When Mercer suggests that McQuebb should take a pair of candlesticks, he offends the burglar's artistic pride. To Mercer's claim that they were made by Paul Revere, McQuebb answers: "As a patriot I salute him, but as an artist . . . ." He explains to Mercer that he has been a burglar in all the best places—Cleveland, Chicago, and "McKeesport, Pennsylvania"—and he does not need advice.

Mercer, however, is victorious. McQuebb has just recently robbed Mercer's brother-in-law, and he and Mercer argue about the address. Schwartz, a policeman with an Irish brogue, arrives and supports Mercer's argument. McQuebb and Mercer had a wager concerning the address; and McQuebb, a bit stuffily, tells Mercer, "I'll send you my check in the morning." After Schwartz leaves, assured by Mercer that everything is all right, Mercer's honest enthusiasm again scores a victory over McQuebb's tired professionalism. Just as the burglar is ready to leave, convinced that he has taken everything of value, Mercer unlocks the wall safe, opening new labors for him. "Oh, for Heaven's sake," McQuebb says, as the curtain starts to fall, "Oh, Lordy, I'll never get home."

In another of these plays, *The Suitor,* Mercer is a young businessman in love with the boss's daughter, again named Genevieve. The skit is built around his attempts to propose to her before leaving for Europe on a business trip. He has only twenty-two minutes to propose and catch his ship; and, since it takes seventeen minutes to arrive at the dock, he has only five minutes with Genevieve. Interruptions from Genevieve's senile grandmother, passing neighbors, and returning parents seem to spell defeat for Mercer. As he starts to leave, however, he calls back to her, "Genevieve!"

She answers, "What, Kenneth?"

"When I come back, will you marry me?"

"Yes, Kenneth."

"All right. Good evening," he calls as the curtain falls; and the mild, ineffectual man is again victorious.

In *The Uncle,* Connelly pits Mercer, here a bachelor, against a sister and her son, Theodore. Both the sister and Theodore are decent people; but they have a knowledge and efficiency that could overwhelm the innocent Mercer—if luck and cunning were not on his side. The skit concerns one evening during which Kenneth has been trapped by his sister, Gertrude, into babysitting with his nephew. Theodore, a serious thirteen-year-old student, is studying Greek, Latin, plane geometry, trigonometry, and "current events." He wants Mercer to help him with his

Greek. Mercer escapes this trap, and the boy then moves to mathematics. Again by a few simple (and perhaps simple-minded) ruses, Mercer escapes. He is, however, willing to be of help with "current events" until Theodore tells him that the assigned topic is "The Political Situation in China"; and Kenneth then sends him to bed—like Thurber's Walter Mitty, with whom he has something in common— "inscrutable to the end."

V   Ex Cathedra: *An Art Play*

In some respects, the Mercer plays might be considered a continuation of Connelly's earlier aim to write plays both popular and significant, with the first concern given to popularity; however, one short play published in 1926 in *Theatre Arts* is a clear demonstration that Connelly was also anxious to try new fields. Just two months before this play was published, John Mason Brown, in surveying the theater season, had listed Connelly among other "established playwrights" who would produce plays "which by their very familiarity [would] insure interested followings."[24] It is to be doubted, however, if either Brown or Connelly would include *Ex Cathedra,* "a monographic pantomime,"[25] in that category of plays.

Ex Cathedra, a narrative drama in pantomime, is set in the sixteenth century; and it has for its central action a clerk's reading of a letter he has written. As he reads, the contents of the letter are acted out in pantomime. The action of the letter concerns a poor, honest merchant who has been selected to play the role of Christ in a town passion play. Although he feels a religious obligation to play the role, the merchant is justly concerned with the dangers. He has taken sanctuary in the church to be safe from his creditors who would seize him and throw him into prison. As the play is to be given on church property, however, he does take the part. A nephew of his creditor, who is to play the role of Judas—a bit of type-casting, as it develops— is in the play only to trap the merchant; and, during the betrayal scene, he pushes the merchant beyond the protection of the church into the hands of the waiting creditors. This "sacrilege" offends the Lord Justice, who not only orders the merchant be set free, but also has him forgiven for his debts.

Looking back from *The Green Pastures,* we might find in this short play Connelly's early concern with religious drama. We might also find in the narration-pantomime technique of *Ex Cathedra* a continuation of Connelly's interest in Expressionism. It would, however, be a mistake to credit Connelly with interests in this play that are not really there. *Ex Cathedra,* it is true, does have a religious subject, but its point of view is humanistic, not religious. The clerk who writes the letter—and thus gives the audience a point of view formally religious—is amused by the episode and seems to be unaware of the relationship between the event and its Biblical parallel; and in spite of the theatrical techniques and the Romantic setting, the play depends upon Realistic theater for its "truth." The action and the meaning of *Ex Cathedra* are not a projection of the inner life of the narrator; instead, they stand, ironically, in contrast to him. Connelly, as a Realist, is pointing to an external action for his meaning.

The technique of a narrator's speaking while the play is performed in pantomime is probably worth more attention than it has received. It foreshadows Wilder's use of a Stage Manager in *Our Town* and the narrative-opening of John VanDruten's *I Remember Mama.* Even though there is something *arty*—rather than artistic—about the device, it did give Connelly a means by which he could speak of religion. If Connelly is seldom mystical in his beliefs, he is always courteous and compassionate in reporting the mystic beliefs of others; and the narrative technique of *Ex Cathedra* allows him to show an action and to comment pleasantly on it while still retaining his distance.

VI   The New Yorker: *Essays and Fiction*

In 1925 Harold Ross, one of the members of The Vicious Circle and a particular friend of Connelly, started *The New Yorker,* a most precarious financial venture; in fact, during the first few years of its existence, the magazine was such a poor risk that established writers like Connelly, Woollcott, and Edna Ferber could have been willing to associate with it only on a personal basis. In the beginning, Connelly and the others were needed by Ross to give the magazine some status. Raoul Fleischmann, Ross's backer, agreed to finance the magazine only if Ross could find some "impressive names to please the [other] backers."[26] Ross turned to the Round Table regulars, and, in addition to Connelly, he succeeded in getting permission to list as his "Advisory Editors," Heywood Broun, Edna Ferber, Kaufman, Alice Duer Miller, Dorothy Parker, and Woollcott; and the first issue of *The New Yorker,* February 21, 1925, carried these names.

As Dale Kramer has pointed out, the amateur interest of the Algonquin Wits in the magazine diminished as their professional obligations to their own careers increased; but "Marc Connelly and Dorothy Parker continued to write for the magazine."[27] Connelly, in fact, is always credited with being one of the more "enthusiastic supporters" of *The New Yorker* during this period. Among his contributions, in addition to the editorial assistance he gave Ross, are a number of essays, skits, travel articles, and satires that indicate the degree of his help and the breadth of his talent.

During 1927, for example, *The New Yorker* published a variety of Connelly's short pieces: "Washington in a Sack Suit," a satire on Calvin Coolidge's philosophy of a business-run government; "Paris, 1927 Style," a satire on Paris as a tourist trap; "Luncheon at Sea," a satiric skit aimed at the Rotary Club; and, at least, three short stories—"Gentleman Returning from a Party," "Barmecide's Feast," and "Happiest Man in the World." In 1928, there was an even wider variety: "The Fable," a medieval romance, rather like *Ex Cathedra;* "A Dear Old Couple," an ironic short story; "Profiles: A Boy in a Barn," a personality sketch about Joe Cook, the "One-Man Vaudeville Show"; "An Hour Before High Noon," a Dorothy Parker kind of short story; "Prominent New Yorkers: Major Fennister," a favorable short biography of a democratic banker; and "A Panic in Hollywood," a satire on the effects of "talking pictures" on the careers of some of the silent-movie actors.[28]

Although Connelly won an O. Henry award for one of his short stories, "Coroner's Inquest," which first appeared in the February 8, 1930, issue of *Collier's,* and although his last major publication, *A Souvenir from Qam* (1964), was a novel, there has been little critical attention paid to his fiction. The neglect does not, however, seem to be a value judgment. Connelly's reputation as a playwright has been so great that most critics have assumed that any work he has done in other forms must have been in the nature of a private avocation. When *A*

Souvenir from Qam was first published, for example, the question most often asked was "why?" rather than "what?" "Why," the reviewers wanted to know, "did a man of seventy-four suddenly turn to fiction?"

Connelly's reputation, to be sure, was built by his playwriting; and, unless there is a drastic change, it will remain a dramatist's reputation. At the same time, however, if Mr. Connelly had never written a play, he would still have some claims to interest from literary historians for his fiction.

VII *The Short Stories*

Connelly wrote short stories for only about five years, starting with "Luncheon at Sea" for *The New Yorker* in 1927 and ending with "Coroner's Inquest" for *Collier's* in 1930. Only five of these stories have been republished since their initial appearance —"Barmecide's Feast," "Coroner's Inquest," and "The Guest," frequently, and "A Dear Old Couple" and "Happiest Man in the World," at least once. We do not intend to suggest that Connelly's fiction, in the context of all his works, should be given major attention; however, it does demonstrate something of the man's literary versatility and throws some light upon his methods of craftsmanship. His fiction, moreover, is bound up in the world of the theater; and an examination of the three best-known short stories is probably of some value.

These three stories—"Barmecide's Feast," "Coroner's Inquest," and "The Guest"—are dramatic in structure and in method. The principal element in each story is dialogue, and each story ends with a "fast curtain" after the last line. "The Guest," in fact, is so obviously in play form that a note in the Modern Library edition warns the reader, "No performance may be given without the permission of the author." Both it and "Coroner's Inquest" have no narrative content at all, beyond the stage directions necessary to describe the action; and, in all three stories, the entire meaning is carried through the dialogue. "Coroner's Inquest" and "The Guest" are much like vaudeville skits, even to an observation of the unities of time and place necessary to the short realistic skit. "Barmecide's Feast" (an imaginary feast for hungry beggars), in its present form, could not be played on the stage; but the other two stories could.

"Barmecide's Feast" deals with a Christmas Eve in the fashionable New York apartment home of Mr. and Mrs. Morton, two successful people who did everything expected of them and on time. They had, on this Christmas Eve, taken care of their shopping list, including gold coins for the servants and toys for the children of friends and servants. They were—in every way that may be measured by a public act—decent people. They felt sympathy for people whose lives were less well-regulated than their own, for people who were less affluent: "People buying presents at the last minute, poor things . . . . Imagine what it must be like down on the East Side." They were sensitive to the feelings of others, realizing, for example, that they should not accept an invitation offered them: "After all it is Christmas Eve and he [the man who invited them] and Marcia would like to be alone even if they didn't say so."

The Mortons were people who in organizing disorder and discomfort out of their lives had made themselves unnecessary to others, and they were bored. They went to the theater, on the one night of the year that the theater is always half-empty. They came home; and, having nothing that needed to be done, they went to bed early. "They fell asleep. It was after midnight and bells began to ring somewhere."

The story, written in a style which has since been described as *"New Yorker,"* is muted throughout, seemingly dramatic in its objectivity, but without an action and without a climax. The theme—that good manners and civilized behavior do not make a Christmas spirit—is suggested throughout the story; but Connelly never once "points the moral." He does not even explain the title or its relationship to the story.

"Coroner's Inquest," in spite of its greater popularity—as evidenced by the O. Henry award and a half-dozen or more republications—is not so good a piece of work, not so moving, nor so skillful as "Barmecide's Feast." Although Mr. Connelly told me that this story "was meant to be grimly tragic," it has a great deal of the "droll story" quality about it. The basic action is centered around a courtroom investigation of the double-murder of two midgets—James Dowle and Theodore Robel. The narrator is Frank Wineguard, the stage manager for *Hello, America* and the employer of the smaller of the two midgets, Dowle. The story is his testimony.

Dowle has been supporting Robel, who, because he has been supposedly going through a "second growth," is unable to find work as a midget. Wineguard explains that he doubted that a real second growth was taking place, but Robel was so depressed that he refused to be measured. The truth—and the point of the story—is that Robel has been lying to Dowle so that in sympathy Dowle will support him. A loss of one's midget status—and thus the ability to work as a performer—seemingly is a common fear of midget entertainers. Robel has been cutting inches off his cane to give the illusion that he is growing. When Dowle discovers the trick, he and Robel kill each other in a knife fight.

"Coroner's Inquest," it is true, deals with betrayal and death; but there is an element of the macabre joke about the entire situation. The pathos of the situation, however, was probably more meaningful in the depression year of 1930.

For "The Guest," Connelly returns once again to Mr. Mercer, his protagonist of such one-act plays as *The Traveler* and *The Bridegroom*. In this episode, Mr. Mercer is the victim of the "customer service" of the North American chain of hotels. Like the protagonist of *Beggar on Horseback*, Mercer finds the multiplication of mechanical gimmicks leads only to the separation of man from his purpose. With the aid of such gimmicks, he is cut off from an important business call, given dog food when he orders coffee, has a full-dress suit delivered to him instead of his own business suit, and finally—clad only in his nightgown—he is "thrown out" of the hotel when he complains about the mistakes.

Like Thurber's Walter Mitty, however, Mr. Mercer is saved from absolute defeat by the audacity of his imagination. When the hotel manager demands the name of his attorney, Mercer replies with a great deal of dignity, "Aussel, Aussel, Coyne, and Mehoff," the business firm with which Mercer lost his appointment through the inefficiency of the hotel. If the manager starts his day with a call to them, Mr. Mercer has some reason to believe that he will not be alone in the street in his nightgown.

What is true of Connelly's drama during these years is also true of his fiction. The central concern of much of his work is with the individual's attempt to defend himself against outside deception and internal fears. For Connelly, the outside deception is of less importance than the internal fears; for fear leads one to sacrifice feeling for comfort, ease, and order. His approach to this problem is often, of necessity, through the joke, the gag, the comic story, the skit; for Connelly views the problem as one that comes from taking one's self—or one's employer, wife, or neighbor—or one's position too seriously. If the immediate objects for Connelly's humor—train service, hotel service, New York apartment dwelling, "show business"—now seem far off in time, his literature for this period is still saved from the museum by his concern with a problem that does not grow old— the mature male's growing fear of being involved in a life that is too complex and too difficult for him.

We do not intend to suggest, however, that Connelly's fiction is concerned only with fear of involvement. In another of his short stories from this period, "Happiest Man in the World," Connelly—using a stream-of-consciousness monologue—shows the jumbled thoughts of a young man who has just become engaged; and the obvious subject of the piece is the "cunning of women." In another short story, "A Dear Old Couple," Connelly—in what is almost an exception for him—puts his focus on the hard of heart. The "Dear Old Couple" are a smug, self-satisfied pair who have just turned out a young couple of servants for "immorality," and now they feel betrayed.

In the main, however, the work of these years was a preparation for *The Green Pastures*. It is true that in none of these works does Connelly deal with Negroes or (with the exception of *Ex Cathedra*) with religion; but Bemis with his aching tooth, Mr. and Mrs. Morton with their empty apartment, and the Wild Man of Borneo all hunger for an invitation to a heavenly fish fry; and their creator makes it obvious that he would like to see them get it. Connelly, with his natural sympathy for the underdog, for the man isolated from his society, eventually had to get to the problem of the Negro.

CHAPTER 4

The Green Pastures

THE GREEN PASTURES is, undoubtedly, among the half dozen or so most respected plays in American dramatic literature. It gave Mr. Connelly an international reputation, a private fortune, and a great deal of personal satisfaction. Unfortunately for his other works, it also gave many theater critics and historians the general impression that Marc Connelly was a one-play author. Such an impression came not merely because *The Green Pastures* is the finest single piece of writing that Mr. Connelly has ever done, but also because, in various superficial ways, it appears to be utterly different from all his other works. It is his only play about Negroes; it is his only full-length play on a religious subject; it is his only play without a conventional happy ending.

I *The Composition and History*

The popularity of *The Green Pastures* is such that the history of the play, from its composition through its long runs both here and in Europe, has become a part of the legend of American drama; it is not too much to argue, in fact, that the "story" surrounding *The Green Pastures* is probably the best-known single piece of theatrical history in America. In 1928, Harper and Brothers published a collection of dialect stories by Roark Bradford, *Ol' Man Adam an' His Chillun,* which was popular immediately with the Broadway literary colony. F. P. Adams, for example, on December 28, 1928, reported to his readers that he had had lunch with Bradford, "the author of my favorite book ... and so to dinner with M. Connelly. ..."[1] This linking of *Ol' Man Adam* and Connelly by Adams was, probably, not accidental. Sometime earlier that year, Rollin Kirby, three-time winner of the Pulitzer Prize for cartooning, had recommended the book to Connelly, who immediately saw dramatic possibilities in its materials; and in 1929, when he went to New Orleans to see Bradford, he wrote "the first act of *The Green Pastures* on the boat S. S. Dixie en route."[2]

Connelly spent considerable time in Louisiana, researching the subject. Bradford's book, as he acknowledged in the preface to the play, had "suggested" the play to him; but, largely, beyond the fact that *Ol' Man Adam* gave Connelly the idea of a Biblical play done in Southern American Negro dialect, *The Green Pastures* owes its literary source to the Old Testament and its diction to Connelly's research on the scene. "I went into the farm country of St. Francis Parish—near Baton Rouge," he wrote of his experiences in Louisiana; ". . . I read my play to sharecroppers."[3] Connelly's ear for oral language, although given little attention in the discussion of his earlier plays, was always one of his great assets as a playwright. Sometimes critics, like John Mason Brown, had complained that his ear for the idiom— "the half-written Algonquins"—led him to sacrifice plotting for tone, theme for "local color"; but, if his friends on Broadway had thought about the problem of research in terms of language, they would have agreed that Connelly was wonderfully trained and admirably suited by talent and interest to make the kind of careful language study that was necessary to give *The Green Pastures* its authenticity.

Mr. Connelly, moreover, had always had a great deal of sensitivity to intent. Charley Bemis in *The Wisdom Tooth,* J. Daniel Thompson in *The Wild Man of Borneo,* and Merton in *Merton of the Movies* are all treated as heroes, not because they perform heroic actions or make heroic speeches, but because, in spite of their doing the weak thing and saying the wrong thing, Connelly "intuits" their good intentions. This sensitivity to intent, as well as Connelly's eye and ear for accurate detail, has made *The Green Pastures* appealing to millions of viewers and readers who have been able to gain from the experiences of the characters some insight into their own lives.

Connelly spent over a year writing the play and then another six months looking for a producer. All of the established New

York producers turned down the play, in spite of Connelly's reputation for commercial success, convinced that, for a variety of reasons, *The Green Pastures* would be "bad business." Few religious plays succeeded at the box office, and, at the time, no play with an all-Negro cast had ever been a good investment. There were, moreover, fears that a play with a Negro actor playing God would offend the white, religious theater-goers. Finally, Rowland Stebbins, a retired stockbroker, made himself a part of American theater history by risking his reputation for financial shrewdness by backing the play.[4] Connelly's casting of the play—especially the selection of Richard B. Harrison to play the Lawd—is almost a separate story, certainly an important episode in the history of the Negro actor in American theater.[5]

The play opened in the Mansfield Theatre in New York on February 26, 1930; and, although there were still a few doubts about the financial future of the play, there were none about its worth as drama. Burns Mantle summed up critical opinion when he wrote of the awarding of the Pulitzer Prize to *The Green Pastures* as the best play of the year: "In the awarding of the prize, not a single dissenting voice was heard, either in the committee or in the press...."[6] *Variety* approved of the play as "art theatre," but expressed doubts that the play would run long in a commercial theater.[7]

Some critics, to be sure, had reservations about certain aspects of *The Green Pastures*. Mantle, for example, felt there was some injustice done to Bradford, who was given credit merely for "the suggestion," rather than as a collaborator. Francis Fergusson, in answering that charge, called *The Green Pastures* "a myth [belonging more to the Bible than to Bradford] which Mr. Connelly discovered nearly intact and devoted himself humbly to translating into stage terms." Fergusson argued that Connelly's discovery of the "truth" in Bradford's "farcical" tales deserved special credit. "Discovery of this kind," he wrote, "... is of course more creative than confecting something supposedly new." Fergusson, however, complained that the "sinful folk" were modeled on "smart Harlemites," rather than on the Louisiana Negro, perhaps unaware that the New Orleans native, of any race, is also metropolitan, "smart." In commenting upon Fergusson's complaint, Mr. Connelly told me, "The Harlem aspect mentioned was an actual attempt to create the atmosphere

I found in the 'barrel-house' in New Orleans." Fergusson's complaint was, moreover, only a qualification; and he approved of Connelly's other characters. "He has managed," Fergusson wrote, "to avoid condescending. . . ."[8]

The Green Pastures and all associated with it have become part of the general cultural history of the 1930's. Mantle, in writing of a new play that Rowland Stebbins produced a dozen years later, for example, identified Stebbins as the man "who will be known to the end of the century as the noble soul who had enough faith in Marc Connelly's 'Green Pastures' to bring it to production after so-called wiser heads of Broadway had neglected to do so."[9] *The Green Pastures* was even given credit for "saving" the reputation of the Pulitzer Prize. In commenting upon other Pulitzer Prize selections for 1929–30, a reviewer for the *Literary Digest* argued that *The Green Pastures* was the only work awarded the prize that year that "No one questions . . . ." All the other Pulitzer choices were challenged, sometimes bitterly. Why should Oliver LaFarge have been selected rather than Hemingway, or Conrad Aiken rather than Elinor Wylie? With obvious approval, the *Literary Digest* concluded its account with a statement from Woollcott's article in the *Morning Telegraph:* " 'The Green Pastures' does not need the Pulitzer Prize, but, oh, how the Pulitzer Prize needs 'The Green Pastures.' "[10]

Perhaps longer than any other twentieth-century American play, *The Green Pastures* was important for its news value alone. In the 1930's, the production of the play, the awarding of the Pulitzer Prize, the suggestion that the play demonstrated an awakened social conscience, the various long-run records that the play established, all were reported with enthusiasm by the press.[11] And then in June, 1935, while the play was still enjoying an unbroken run throughout the United States, Warner Brothers purchased the film rights to it on terms that "were all Connelly's." He directed it, staged it, cast it. The success of the film not only helped to make Connelly "the highest paid" writer in Hollywood, but it also spread the fame of *The Green Pastures*.

In 1951, Connelly again staged *The Green Pastures* in New York. It opened at the Broadway Theatre March 15 and closed April 21. "No amount of enthusiasm on the part of the individual critic, including this editor," John Chapman wrote of that production, "could make this American miracle play stick. Modern Broadway was just not interested in de Lawd, Gabriel, and the fish-loving angels."[12] Although in one respect *The Green Pastures* on the professional stage is past history at the moment, the play still has its supporters by the thousands, men like John Mason Brown, who, as late as 1963, summed up his critical opinion with this statement: "Let's face it with proper gratitude. *The Green Pastures* is a masterpiece."[13]

For the past two decades, however, there has been a general feeling that the play is too simple for complex academic criticism, too soft for an age of revolution, and perhaps too patronizing for the new role of the Negro in the United States, too much like *Uncle Tom's Cabin*. Just a few years ago, for example, the Bishop of the African Methodist Episcopal Church charged that the play was "irreligious" and "perpetuated outmoded stereotypes" of Negroes.[14] As these various comments indicate, much of the existing criticism of the play has been concerned with its stage history rather than with its literary merit and ideational content. A recent edition of *The Green Pastures*, with sensible, religious essays by W. R. Matthews, John Macmurray, and Henry Self,[15] gives hope that a new interest in the play—a critical interest—is coming into being.

II   *Critical Status*

The tremendous success of the play in the theater, strangely enough, seems to have discouraged serious dramatic criticism about the merits of the play as literature, to a large degree, perhaps, because its "literary merit" was never questioned. Most critics have been content merely to state a verdict. Joseph Wershba, for example, has said that for this play alone Connelly has "assured himself a lasting place in American drama . . .";[16] and this judgment has been rendered hundreds of times. *The Green Pastures*, which has been republished in at least thirty-three different anthologies in the past thirty-seven years, is the one play by Connelly that has never, except for minor cavils, been criticized for artistic "faults."

During the past twenty-five years, however, it has become the fashion to praise the play for what it was, not for what it is. John Gassner, for example, calls *The Green Pastures*, "a play that is inscribed in the permanent records of the American theatre." His critical discussion of the play, however, is limited to a short statement concerned with the difficulty of classifying it: "*The Green Pastures* is unique; it cannot be placed in any existing classification without some reservations. . . . Is there no discrepancy between the 'Harlem' scene and the spirit of the play? Is the play entirely free from a spirit of condescension toward primitive folk and their notions? Yet one cannot overlook the tremendous fascination the play exerted for years after it opened on Broadway. It seemed the culmination of everything we considered a movement toward folk drama for at least a decade, and it was also the only religious drama anyone succeeded in making tolerable to the American public since Charles Rann Kennedy's old-fashioned morality play, *The Servant in the House.*"[17]

E. Bradlee Watson and Benfield Pressey also defend the play in historical terms: ". . . *The Green Pastures* . . . seems itself both miraculous and inevitable—miraculous because it arose out of such unpredictable comings-together; inevitable because by 1930 the theatre in America was overripe for a great Negro play and a great religious play. . . . Unconsciously . . . America needed *The Green Pastures.*" In judging the play as living dramatic literature, however, they are less certain: although ". . . it remains a monumental attainment in the American theatre," they write, ". . . it is not likely to be often available in revivals. . . ."[18]

The Green Pastures, to be sure, is an expensive play to stage; but the modern reader still finds it an exciting experience, not merely an historical monument. In an interview with Ward Morehouse in 1951, following its last full-scale professional revival, Connelly said of the play: "I'm glad that the critics find it a simple play. I feel that it is offered as an honest inquiry into man's attempt to find dignity and virtue within himself, that it invites introspection and a search for old dignities."[19]

III *The Play*

The Green Pastures is not a play utterly different from everything that Connelly had done before; *The Deep Tangled Wildwood, The Wisdom Tooth,* and *The Wild Man of Borneo,* for examples, are quite obviously searches for "old dignities." What distinguishes *The Green Pastures* from these earlier plays is its scope. In this play Connelly selected his materials, not from minor aspects of contemporary society, but from the central religious-philosophical myth of Western civilization, the Hebraic-Christian accounts in the Bible; and he then applied some of the implications of that myth to one group of suffering American humanity, the Southern Negro.

The play[20] is divided into two parts: the first, in ten scenes; the second, in eight. The first part opens in a Negro Sunday School in New Orleans, where the kindly preacher, Mr. Deshee, is beginning a study of the Bible for his young charges. Although, seemingly, the selection of the Biblical episodes—life in Heaven before creation, the creation of Adam and Eve, the fall of Cain, and the Noah story—merely follow a chronological account, they have a thematic purpose: they deal with a theory of human reformation. They present, from the Lawd's point of view, a theory of crime and punishment. Man—especially starting with Cain—has sinned; and with the flood, he has been punished. The new world—that is "startin' all over again"—is founded only by the virtuous, the chosen few who survived the flood.

Many of Connelly's earlier plays stopped at this point, the moment of the new start; but quite obviously, in the context of *The Green Pastures,* a good life created by the "remaining virtuous" is too narrow a view of man to succeed. It is not merely that the first part ends with God saying softly, "I only hope it's goin' to work out all right"; it is, also, that Gabriel, while still respectful of the Lawd, has "no enthusiasm" for the success of the project.

In the second part of *The Green Pastures,* the materials are selected from episodes in the Bible from the story of Moses to the fall of Jerusalem; and, upon first observation, the second part seems merely to repeat the theme of the first: man, in spite of God's help, again proves incapable of reform. This time, God does not punish with a flood, but with a renunciation. Quite obviously, the history of man, from the Lawd's point of view, demonstrates that mankind is incapable of being "worthy of de breath I gave you."

Starting with the sixth scene of Part Two, however, *The Green Pastures* moves from a concern with the "reformation" of man to a concern with the "nature" of man. The question is no longer, "How can man be reformed?"; instead, it becomes, "What is man?" In the seventh scene, the Lawd gets a suggestion of an answer to that second question: man is a creature full of weaknesses, but he tries. He has hope in the midst of catastrophe, courage in the midst of despair, and compassion in the midst of suffering. And he learned to be so wise "Through sufferin'," as Hezdrel tells God.

God, when He comes to understand His own creation, learns the lesson: even a God must suffer, must be involved with mankind as man is. *The Green Pastures* ends in the spectacle of Christ on the cross; and the "Voice," man, learns not to behave differently, but to feel beyond himself. The play ends with the extension of human sympathy to a suffering God: "Oh, dat's a terrible burden [involvement with suffering mankind, as well as the cross] for one man to carry!" As Vincent Long comments in his "Introduction" to the play, however we start our association with *The Green Pastures*—with "amusement" or with "indulgent condescension"—"We soon find ... that we are entering into an experience of real religion."[21]

The "religious truth" of the play is not, however, concerned with a question of theology. It is, rather, concerned with man's relationship to man. If, the play seems to ask, even with a just God, man sins but is yet redeemed because he knows suffering and has learned mercy, how should men treat each other? Specifically, the question raised for an American audience centers around the attitude the fortunate white-American theater-goers should have toward "the least of these, thy brothers."

IV   The Use of Sentimentality

Modern Negroes, weary of the "Uncle Tom" picture of the "Good Ol' Darky," may be offended at the opening scene of *The Green Pastures*. Although Mr. Deshee is shown as a good man, he is a kind of "Uncle Tom," a man who *seems* so simple that his goodness appears to be the result of simple-mindedness rather than of virtue. In the first Sunday School scene, for example, he is teaching a class of small Negro children. In his opening speech, he summarizes the first five chapters of Genesis; and the emphasis is entirely upon long life: "Adam lived a hundred an' thirty years an' begat a son in his own likeness . . . Seth. An de' days of Adam after he had begotten Seth were eight hundred years!" The only reference to contemporary life is that "ol' Mrs. Gurney's mammy" is called "ol' Mrs. Methusaleh caize she's so ol'." This summary, with its list of *begats* and *deaths,* Mr. Deshee calls "de meat and substance" of the first five books; and he concludes his lesson with the question, "Now, how you think you gonter like de Bible?"

All questions from the children are answered with a proper respect for conventional morality and a dependence upon the literal truth of the Bible as Mr. Deshee understands it. In the third scene, for example, one boy wants to be certain that Adam and Eve had been married a proper length of time before the birth of Cain. "My mammy say it was a hund'ed years," the boy says. Mr. Deshee admits that it is now difficult to be exact about the number of years, but his answer assures the boy that at least the proper number of months had passed.[22]

This concern with age and with proper behavior seems to suggest a lack of understanding of the "central truths" of the religious story, at least from the view of modern, educated Americans in the 1930's. Mr. Deshee, however, is not ignorant of life. As the spiritual leader of a people who live hungry, die young, and face day-after-day indictments that they are "by nature" immoral, Mr. Deshee's concern with age and conventional behavior is part of an attempt to translate the abstract religion into a practical guide. A people who die young must be impressed by old age.

Connelly avoids making obvious social-protest associations. Mr. Deshee's life among the poor, the hungry, and the shamed —the Negro scene—is never mentioned. Rather a kindly, old preacher and a chorus of innocent children set the stage. No one, whatever his racial opinions, would deny the basic goodness of such people; but the audience's sympathy for this group must also be mixed with some mild, sophisticated contempt. Undoubtedly in such a state, the folk are good; but the suggestion is that "such a state" is, therefore, necessary for them.

The first scene in Heaven, the second scene of Part One, develops the same concept of the good, simple "Darky" and suggests the kind of state necessary for his goodness. This scene does show "adults"—Angels, God, Gabriel; but the notion of their "simple goodness" is strengthened by their childlike responses and by the fact that, in terms of the religious story used, they are naturally good. Connelly, moreover, surrounds them with children, Cherubs. The use of characters who conform to the stereotype of the "good Darky" and who are yet loosely drawn from the Biblical story makes a sentimental appeal to the audience. Showing the "naturally" good, simple Negro in his pursuit of "naturally" good, simple goals reinforces a sentimental view with a religious overtone. The normal audience response, it seems to me, is largely sentimental; but there must also be the slightly uncomfortable feeling that this sentiment has the support of powerful forces.

V *The Harlem Evil*

In the following scenes—with Cain, with the blues-singing Zeba, with the Children of Noah, with the Children of Israel, and in the "Harlem" scenes that Francis Fergusson and John Gassner did not like—the Lawd and the audience have another view of man, the Negro. To some degree, the desired response is also to a stereotype: the Negro as naturally violent and naturally brutal. The evidence offered is overwhelming. He is a "depraved being" capable of any crime: he kills his brother, he steals, he lies, he betrays. He does, in fact, everything that all the imperfect heroes and villains of the Old Testament did; and he does it all in a fashion that will allow those who view the Negro actors in the play to conclude that what is being shown is a Realistic portrayal of "Negro behavior."

The uneasiness of those who would like *The Green Pastures* to be a propaganda piece for the Negro—both white critics in the early 1930's and Negro leaders in the 1950's and 1960's—is a clear demonstration that Connelly did his work well. The audience is ready to join the Lawd in His weariness with sin. "Dat's about enough," the Lawd announces. "I's stood all I kin from you. I tried to make dis a good earth. I helped Adam, I helped Noah, I helped Moses, an' I helped David. What's de grain dat grew out of de seed? Sin! Nothin' but sin throughout de whole world. . . . So I renounce you. Listen to the words of yo' Lawd God Jehovah, for dey is de last words yo' ever hear from me. I repent of dese people dat I have made and I will deliver dem no more."

Connelly's insight into the nature of the "Good Outsider," weary with the "transgressions of the folk," seems so fresh that this characterization might have been created in the 1960's, rather than in 1930, as the play relates to the race problem in the United States. White Americans still complain that the Negro drive for "equal rights" is moving too fast, some evidence perhaps of a repentance of past "deliverances."

The accumulative view of these central scenes of the play contrasts with the first three scenes and shows the Negro as violent and depraved. At first, a sentimental solution seems suggested; for, if the Negro could move back to the world of Mr. Deshee's Sunday School and the Heavenly fish fry, there would be no necessity to deal with the world of Cain and Harlem; however, the Lawd, like the audience, must contemplate punishment and desertion as the answer.

VI   *The Reconciliation*

With the Lawd's renunciation scene, however, a pronounced change takes place in the tone of the play and in the response from the audience. Until the last few scenes, the white, sophisticated audience has been watching—with some amusement, some sympathy, and probably some impatience—the history of "the folk" from the point of view of the Lawd. In another place,[23] I have argued that, in spite of the fact that the Lawd was played by a Negro actor, his character, in part, is based on a stereotype of the "Good White Man," as he sees himself in relationship to the folk. There may be some question as to the validity of that argument, but there is little to the assumption that the Lawd in his renunciation speech reflects the varied attitudes of well-meaning, sympathetic, tired outsiders to the problems and errors of the folk.

From the moment of renunciation, however, the Lawd, in dramatic terms, loses his superiority. In the sixth scene of Part Two the Lawd recognizes the righteousness of Hosea, now a resident of Heaven, although Hosea obviously disagrees with the Lawd's renunciation. He becomes the Lawd's superior, and in their conflict—an unspoken *agon*—Hosea overwhelms the Lawd.

The Lawd's final speech in this scene shows his capitulation to a superior force. "You know I said I wouldn't come down," the Lawd shouts down to the voice of goodness on earth after Hosea's silence has weakened his resolve. "Why don't he answer me a little? Listen, I'll tell you what I'll do. I ain't goin' to promise you anythin', and I ain't goin' to do nothin' to help you. I'm just feelin' a little low, an' I'm only comin' down to make myself feel a little better, dat's all."

In the last dramatic scene of the play, the Lawd comes in conflict with Hezdrel, one of the characters Connelly created without Biblical authority. If the characters to this point in the play can be divided into "good, simple" and "bad, smart-alecky Harlem" Negroes, Hezdrel is something new. He is good, courageous, faithful, but he is also a complicated human being, wiser in the matters of man than the Lawd himself. The Lawd, in fact, finally has to ask Hezdrel for the secret of knowledge— how does one (even God) discover mercy? Hezdrel's answer— "Through suffering"—leaves the Lawd confused, but full of admiration. The Lawd is now an "inferior being" who must be removed from the scene of the heroic action for his own safety. He can be only a supporting character as He leaves the heroic Hezdrel, giving the battle cry of man, "Give 'em eve'ything, Boys."

In these two scenes, the audience's sympathy must shift from the Lawd to Hosea and Hezdrel. They are, in terms of *The Green Pastures,* morally superior. They hold, in terms of their *agons* with the Lawd, the same position that Tiresias holds against Oedipus, Antigone against Creon: they are right. At this point, the audience must become aware that, although the actors are Negroes, the subject is man; and the Lawd's renunciation of "dese people" includes not merely the *folk* in the play, but the folk in the audience.

The identification of the audience with the Lawd has now ceased. The history of the play is no longer a Negro history, but the history of Hebraic-Christian man. If the white outsider continues in his sympathy with the Lawd's decision to withdraw from the Negro world, he must put himself in a world from which God has withdrawn, and he must approve of that withdrawal. The sophisticated audience has been sentenced by its own biases to a God-forsaken world.

The Lawd of *The Green Pastures* concludes that He cannot judge men fairly from without, and the play ends with the sacrifice of Jesus on the cross. Whether this is orthodox Christian doctrine or not is a matter for theologians,[24] but from a dramatic point of view, Connelly's *The Green Pastures* offers a successful pattern for the writer of folk drama. He starts with the biases for and against the folk, and he forces his audience to examine these biases and their assumptions not only about the "folk" but about themselves. Once we are caught up in *The Green Pastures*, it is difficult to refuse Connelly's invitation to introspection.

CHAPTER 5

To Fresh Woods and New Fields

WHEN the decade of the 1930's started, America was at the bottom of a depression of fear, confusion, and want. Marc Connelly, in contrast, was in the midst of his greatest period of certainty, order, and plenty. There is something ironic about the fact that the liberal, socially conscious Mr. Connelly should find literary prosperity at the very time the United States discovered the depression; but, as far as his reputation is concerned, 1930 still remains his *annus mirabilis*—the year he won the Pulitzer Prize in drama for *The Green Pastures,* achieved an O. Henry Award in fiction, and joined the ranks of America's greatest playwrights.

Judging his career solely from the bias of the literary critic, one is likely to conclude that, after *The Green Pastures,* Mr. Connelly's career went into a decline. During the years from 1930 to the outbreak of World War II, Mr. Connelly wrote only a few dramatic works that are now generally available—*The Farmer Takes a Wife,* a full-length play written in collaboration with Frank Elser; and two one-act plays, *Little David,* a scene removed from the stage version of *The Green Pastures,* and *The Mole on Lincoln's Cheek,* a radio play—and none of these works is of the same merit as *Merton of the Movies* or *The Wisdom Tooth.* Obviously, therefore, critics of the time who were waiting for another *Green Pastures* were disappointed; and some were even convinced that Mr. Connelly had retired from literature.

Viewing Connelly as an artist-in-action rather than as a writer-in-print, however, one could argue that this period was one in which he moved to fresh fields beyond the green pastures and that in the area of American culture, if not in literature, he was more active during these years than he had been even during the 1920's. During this period, he probably wrote more that was produced, if we include his motion picture writing, than during any other period in his life; he was more active in dramatic productions; and he had a more powerful voice in literary matters.

I   *Still* The Green Pastures

The success of *The Green Pastures* gave Connelly a position as a dedicated artist in American letters. Social critics like Heywood Broun found in the play an argument for racial understanding. Even Americans, he wrote, "... who will not sit in the same street car ... with the black," have been reminded by *The Green Pastures* that "... the Negro played a vital part in bringing back to current Christianity its kindliness."[1] One academic critic, Robert Wilkington, found in the play a similarity to the Corpus Christi plays; and he thought the observation to be worthy of attention by other academicians.[2] Connelly, who—except for the interest *Theatre Arts* gave to *Ex Cathedra*—had been generally ignored by the art critics, was now called upon to make pronouncements on "the future of the theatre" in such essays as his "We're Going To Have Better Plays"[3] and in such public addresses as his "Confidence in Survival of American Theatre" speech before the Academy of Theatre Arts.[4]

The Green Pastures continued to be almost a full-time occupation for Connelly for the first half of the decade. In 1930, the play ran in New York. In 1931, it completed its first run with six hundred and forty performances; and then it moved to Chicago for the 1931–32 season. In Chicago, it ran for nineteen weeks and was easily the city's most important theater event of the year. In 1932, it started a long successful tour of the United States that continued until 1935, when it returned to New York with a record of 1,642 continuous performances. Its second New York run ended with seventy-three performances in March, 1935, only because of the death of Richard B. Harrison, that remarkable actor who played De Lawd. With Harrison's death, the unbroken run of *The Green Pastures* came to an end; but Connelly spent the next ten years looking for another such man to play the role. In 1944, he told Ward Morehouse, "If I could find the actor needed for 'The Green Pastures,' I would start producing the play next month, or next week—or tomorrow."[5]

If it seems difficult in this survey of Connelly's literary life to move beyond *The Green Pastures,* the problem is inherent in the subject. Anyone assessing Connelly's literary and theatrical career in this period is bound to have a distorted notion. Connelly gave more of himself in the 1930's to *The Green Pastures* than to any other single work. Burns Mantle, in 1935, complained that Connelly ". . . is pretty hard to interest [in writing or theater] since the success of 'The Green Pastures' has made him financially independent";[6] but it is difficult to accept this judgment even if we ignore the constant attention which *The Green Pastures* required.

Connelly certainly was not in retirement as far as the "public welfare" was concerned. Unlike his one-time friend, Robert Sherwood, who became so interested in the work of the Roosevelt administration that "his writing suffered a marked decline,"[7] Connelly never became a professional politician. He was, however, active. In 1940, he was among the first to urge Franklin D. Roosevelt to run for a third term. He was president of the Authors' League of America. He spoke often on the relationship of art and the law, protesting, for example, the Chicago ban on Jack Kirkland's adaptation of Erskine Caldwell's *Tobacco Road.* He did a considerable amount of work for fairer copyright laws. At the same time, however, he did not subordinate his writing to his political and social beliefs. Caspar H. Nannes in his *Politics in American Drama* lists only one of Connelly's plays as "projecting a political attitude";[8] and that play, *The Flowers of Virtue,* was not written until 1941.

II *Man of the Theater*

Mantle's suggestion that Connelly was living in near-retirement was a standard one. The picture of Connelly as an easy-going, gifted, but unhurried artist had wide acceptance even among Connelly's close friends, who should have known better. Woollcott, for example, described Connelly's work habits in 1935 in an essay that he thought would be acceptable to his friend: "According to all the legends of Broadway, he [Connelly] is so infuriating a blend of poet, peacock, and procrastinator that any manager ... might reasonably boggle on the brink of an experience likely to unhinge his reason, or at least fray his nerves." At the same time, Woollcott argued that Connelly "brings richer gifts to the theatre than all the other contemporary American playwrights put together"[9]—no mean compliment when we consider that among these contemporaries were Eugene O'Neill, Maxwell Anderson, Robert Sherwood, and Thornton Wilder.

Connelly, who was annoyed at Woollcott's assessment,[10] has always been less concerned with his "gifts" than with his labors. He has frequently told reporters that he does not write easily. As recently as 1965, for example, he told Harry Altschuler, "Even writing a simple declarative sentence is pretty hard."[11] He has, moreover, always had more than a writer's interest in theater. It is entirely in character that he started his career in McKeesport by writing, staging, and acting in his own plays. Throughout his career, he has often acted in his own plays, especially in out-of-town tryouts; and, as a theater director, he was so accomplished that Elliot Nugent and James Thurber wanted him to direct their play, *The Male Animal*.[12] To friends like Woollcott, Connelly's concern with theater may have seemed "peacockish," but for Connelly, drama has always been essentially theater. His complaint against drama critics, in general, is that they do not understand theater. "Nine out of ten of them," he once told Naomi Jolles, "haven't the faintest idea of what actual chemicals are being used on that unseen laboratory of the stage so that nothing gets in the way of a play coming over the footlights."[13]

Connelly, most of the time, has no serious quarrel with the Broadway legend that shows him as a wit, a genial fellow, and a "dewdrop man." He has earned that reputation with years of pranks and droll stories, with a lifetime dedicated to demonstrating that life can be a pleasant, exciting experience. At the same time, he sees no conflict between the enjoyment of life and the amount of work that a man does. In fact, it is sometimes difficult for him to give a proper evaluation of a work done by a man who has not learned to enjoy life. He has, for example, a great deal of sympathy, or more properly, *pity*, for Eugene O'Neill the man; and this pity has, perhaps, stood between him and O'Neill's plays. Connelly's conviction that a man has almost an obligation to find pleasure in life is, undoubtedly, the basis of the general belief shared by many of his friends before *The Green Pastures* that he lacked the "introspection" necessary to write a play with such depth. Connelly is not unaware of "the human condition." Rather, he is aware that he is part of that condition; and he does his best to improve the lot of man by whatever work is at hand.

During the period of the 1930's when, by common consent, he was "pretty hard to interest," Connelly did enough work in the theater and in motion pictures to have made a professional reputation for himself even if he had never written *The Green Pastures.* His discovery, production, and direction of Arthur Kober's *Having Wonderful Time,* for example, earned for him such respect that twenty years later, Joseph Wershba could still comment that, on the basis of that work alone, Connelly could have made "a permanent place for himself" in American drama as a director.[14]

As the director and producer, as well as the author, of *The Green Pastures,* Connelly showed that in all aspects of theater, he was a hard-working, dedicated man. He not only shepherded the play on its tours, but he also directed the motion-picture version of it and took a personal responsibility for the actors. Even when he was working with unsuccessful plays, no critic complained that he was derelict in his duties. John Mason Brown, for example, in a generally unfavorable review of *Everywhere I Roam*—a play about Johnny Appleseed by Arnold Sundgaard that Connelly revised, directed, and staged—commented on "Mr. Connelly's ever-sensitive direction."[15]

In addition to his work with stage plays in New York, Connelly, moreover, was active in motion-picture work in Hollywood. He wrote parts or all of a dozen or so screenplays, including *Cradle Song* (1933), *The Green Pastures* (1935), *The Farmer Takes a Wife* and *Captains Courageous* (both in 1937), and *I Married a Witch* and *Reunion* (both in 1942).[16] Connelly now jokes about the television reruns of some of his old movies: "They aren't revivals—they're exhumations";[17] but students of the motion picture list these titles among the best work done in the Hollywood of the 1930's.

III   *But as a Playwright*

From 1930 to 1941, Connelly had only two stage plays produced—*The Farmer Takes a Wife* in 1934 and *Everywhere I
Roam* in 1937. He also had two short plays published—*Little
David* in 1937 and *The Mole on Lincoln's Cheek* in 1939. As
far as the public record is concerned, this is Connelly's literary
output for these years. During this time, however, he also copyrighted three other plays—*The Unemployed Ghost* (1931) and
The Little Duchess (1934), one-act plays; and *The Land of
the Living* (1938), a full-length play which, after some revision,
did have an unsuccessful production in 1958 in London under
the title *Hunter's Moon*. When compared with his first twelve
years as a successful playwright, from *Dulcy* through *The Green
Pastures,* this period for Connelly as a writer for the stage is not
impressive; but neither is it a period of retirement.

IV   *The Return of Mr. Mercer*

Connelly's two unpublished, one-act plays of this period—
The Unemployed Ghost[18] and *The Little Duchess*[19]—are much
like the earlier Kenneth Mercer skits: elaborate hoaxes about
the theater, its people, and its jokes. In fact, in *The Unemployed Ghost,* Kenneth Mercer again appears as the protagonist, now, like Connelly himself in 1931, married and honeymoon-
ing in Europe. The action deals with Mercer's adventures in an
English castle that he is investigating as a gift for his bride, who
is in Paris. In the opening scene, Mercer is speaking to his bride
on the phone, when the connection is broken as the first ghost,
J. T. Wissey, appears.
   "You're an American, aren't you," Mercer asks the ghost.
   "Well, I was an American," Wissey agrees.
   "Turned English, huh," Mercer replies.
   Mercer accepts Wissey and his two comrades—Senator Colofort and Mr. Fessenden—as genuine ghosts. Colofort was for-
merly a Senator from California; and Fessenden was Charles I,
but a young lady ghost took his body and left her own, so he is,
now, only the head of Charles I. Mercer is sympathetic with
Fessenden's problem; and, when the ghost tells him the lady will
not return his body because "she's infatuated with" it, Mercer

suggests that Fessenden, too, might find some "fun" in the exchange. "It is no fun for a gentleman," the ghost tells him.

The basic "gag" of the skit is built around the problem of unemployment among ghosts, a matter of serious concern among the living in those first frightened years of the 1930's. There are, Wissey tells Mercer, "eight million of us out of work" in England alone; ". . . there's no call for haunted houses, and most of us are starving to life." In America, the situation is even worse. All the spirits are either trying to "ghost" a book for Admiral Byrd, or to get work as a control for a living medium. A medium who died in New York, Mercer is told, died of "over-population." "Thirty-four thousand Indian controls" were fighting each other to get into her act.

The three ghosts are finally expelled from the castle by a fourth ghost, the "legal" resident; and, when Mercer is able to reach his bride by phone, he reports, "Say this is the GOD-DAMNEDEST castle," just as the curtain falls.

The Little Duchess is, basically, a burlesque of the sentimental rags-to-riches comedy. The Duke, Lord Killwater, has married Cecily Crumb, a charwoman, following a drunken spree. Cecily, to be sure, is an unusual charwoman, as the Duke observes, beautiful and cultured in her speech; but the butler points out that such evidence is no longer valid since Shaw's *Pygmalion* has taught any maid how to be a lady. The gags are still 1920 Broadway. When the Duke tells Cecily, on the morning after the marriage, that he will stick with his bargain because he is a gentleman, and "when a gentleman makes a bargain, no matter how bad it is, he sticks to it," she replies in kind: "I am a Crumb. And a Crumb does the same thing."

The villain of the piece is Lord Tareyton, who arrives to save the Duke, only to discover that the Duchess is his lost love, whom he deserted in World War I. The Duke would sacrifice his own happiness for the woman he loves. "As a rule," he tells Tareyton, "we Killwaters don't give up our wives so easily as this. It is only because you are an old friend of the family."

With the aid of a bottle of wine containing "a strong aphrodisiac," however, Killwater tricks Tareyton into revealing himself as a cad; and, as the curtain falls, Lady Killwater is ordering another bottle of the same wine for her honeymoon supper with Lord Killwater.

V   *One Broadway Success*

The only one of Connelly's full-length plays written in this period that has been taken seriously by theater historians is *The Farmer Takes a Wife;*[20] and, for a variety of reasons associated with the composition of the play, both theater historians and critics have never been quite certain about what Connelly's role was in the writing of it. The play is based on the novel, *Rome Haul,* by Walter D. Edmonds; and, before Connelly even began work on *The Farmer Takes a Wife,* one version, titled *Low Bridge,* had been produced by "... two midwestern universities and one semi-amateur company...."[21] The first version was written by Frank D. Elser, the man now credited with being the co-author of *The Farmer Takes a Wife.*

Theater commentators—perhaps still feeling that Connelly had not given sufficient credit to *Ol' Man Adam* for *The Green Pastures*—were quick to assign credit for *The Farmer Takes a Wife* to Edmonds and Elser. One reviewer, in commenting on this play, noted that Connelly had "reduced" *The Green Pastures* "to stage form" which "netted him something like $500,000 ..."; and then he complained about Connelly's "translating other men's books into Broadway plays."[22] Mantle, who named the work one of the *Best Plays of 1934–35,* listed it as "By Frank D. Elser"; and in his introductory remarks he suggested that Connelly did little more than routine play-doctoring work with Elser's script.

The Farmer Takes a Wife is, however, as much Connelly's work as *Romeo and Juliet* is Shakespeare's. *Rome Haul,* it is true, is the source book for the play; and Elser did bring a play, *Low Bridge,* to Connelly and ask his help in revising it for Broadway. The problem, then, is to determine how much of the final play Elser wrote and how much of it was taken directly from *Rome Haul.*

Elser's part in the composition of *A Farmer Takes a Wife* is, thanks to Mr. Connelly's recent testimony, easy to determine. Elser, who died the week following the closing of the play, in January, 1935, was practically unknown in the theater. While a city editor on the New York *Times,* he had adapted Liam O'Flaherty's *Mr. Gilhooley,* which, while it got some favorable reviews,[23] was not commercially successful. Nonetheless, he resigned from the *Times* to give his full attention to playwriting.[24]

He obtained an option from Edmonds for a dramatization of *Rome Haul*. The result, *Low Bridge,* was, as Mantle commented, "variously produced by those organizations that decorate the fringe of the theatre."[25] Elser, however, was dissatisfied with the play he had written. He took his script of *Low Bridge* to Connelly and asked him if he would collaborate on a new version. While Connelly was considering the matter, Edmonds told him that Elser's option was about to expire; and, if Connelly would wait a few weeks, he would give him exclusive rights to dramatize *Rome Haul.*

"This didn't seem fair to me," Mr. Connelly told me. Elser, who was five years Connelly's senior, had invested a considerable amount of time and energy in *Low Bridge.* If he now had no part in the play that was to open in New York, his hopes for a playwriting career would be ended. At the same time, however, Connelly wanted to work alone. He therefore agreed to do the play if he had complete authority over every detail of the composition and production, and Elser readily assented. Although *The Farmer Takes a Wife* opened in New York in 1934 as written by "Frank D. Elser and Marc Connelly," it would have been the same play if Connelly had accepted Edmonds' offer of exclusive rights. In truth, this play and *Low Bridge* do have much in common, but they are largely alike in the materials taken from the novel.

In writing *The Farmer Takes a Wife,* Connelly returned to the novel for his material, even making visits to the canal area of New York state for firsthand observations; however, although in terms of basic setting, action, and characters, the play is taken from *Rome Haul,* it is not, in any narrow sense of the word, a "dramatization" of the novel. *Rome Haul* is concerned with the development of a practical, realistic moral code by one man, Dan'l Harrow; and this code is set in contrast to the doctrine of respectability in middle-class America. Harrow comes to his private code on the Erie Canal in the mid-nineteenth century, and his code includes a sympathy for those who operate outside the legal and moral rules of conventional society—that society "inland" from the canal. Dan'l, for example, favors the highwayman over the law, the dishonest preacher over his congregation, the half-harlot riverboat cooks over the "respectable" women of inland America. Because he must finally leave the canal and the people he respects—including his own cook, Molly—to return to the land, *Rome Haul* is, in a sense, a tragic book about the loss of independence of spirit on the American frontier. But *The Farmer Takes a Wife,* as Mantle noted, is a happy, romantic story of a "cook-lady who loved the canal and a young farmer ... who was determined that she should forget it." For this play, Connelly took his materials from *Rome Haul* —the language, appearance, and adventures of the "canawlers" —but, as Mantle commented, merely "to provide the decoration...."[26]

As his only new full-length play produced in this period, *The Farmer Takes a Wife* looms larger than it should in the public reputation of Marc Connelly. The play, however, does have merits that have been largely ignored. It is a well-constructed comedy with interesting character types; and, if there is little to tempt the literary critic concerned with theme, the play is still a model of the well-made comedy.

VI The Farmer Takes a Wife

Connelly selected from Edmonds' novel three basic conflicts for his play—one romantic (which he sentimentalized), one melodramatic, and one ideational. All else in *Rome Haul* was subordinated or discarded by the playwright. The central struggle of the play is no longer between two ways of life but is between Dan'l Harrow's love of the land and Molly's love of the canal; and this *agon* is treated in gentle, sentimental terms. The two lesser conflicts—the melodramatic struggle between Dan'l and Klore, Molly's old boatman; and the ideational conflict between the old way (the canal) and progress (the railroad) —are used only as they contribute to the resolution of the central romantic conflict.

Every action of the play is sentimentalized. Connelly discarded those elements from Edmonds' story—most of the sinning, most of the violence, and all of the moral problems—that would mar the nostalgic tone of the play. In contrast to her prototype in the novel, Molly is a young innocent girl, who is protected even on the canal by the fact that she served as her father's cook. She is, when the play opens, cooking for Klore; but his attraction for her has nothing to do with lust or an admiration for violence.

Rather, she is proud of her cooking; and Klore's appetite is the most suitable outlet for her talent. Dan'l is a young man who is working on the canal only as a means of buying a farm. He is conservative, but not tightfisted as he is in the novel. He is brave; however, he does not need to overcome his fears as the Dan'l of the novel does. He is a man with a clear-cut purpose; in fact, he is a great deal more like Dulcy's husband in Connelly's first successful play than like Edmonds' hero.

The first act of the play suggests the canal as a kind of Eden of movement and happy eccentricity. The characters are introduced, and the conflicts are suggested. Connelly's fine hand for witty dialogue is seen in this act, as it is throughout the play; for example, Fortune Friendly, a former preacher and gambler turned dentist, has just pulled two teeth for a "fancy woman," Ivy Elliott. When Fortune is asked about his occupation, he answers: "I gave up preaching to be a dentist and the first patient is a Magdalen from a parlor house." The line in an early draft read *woman* rather than *Magdalen,* but Connelly changed the word in the copyright manuscript. It is the aptness of expression rather than the "tragic issues" of the action that interests Connelly in this play; and his chief concern, it seems safe to conclude, was in giving the proper tone to the work.

Molly and Dan do not enter the scene until midway through the first act, but the early part of the act is largely intended to prepare for their entrance; and their first meeting does little more than suggest their essential purity and their natural attraction to one other. The second act is divided into two scenes, the first a Utica street scene in May and the second a cabin on the *Sarsey Sal,* Dan'l's boat, in September. In the first scene, Dan'l and Molly meet again, just at the moment when she is angry. Klore's drinking is making him an unsuitable man for whom to cook. Dan'l asks her to marry him, but she postpones her answer because she does not want to leave the canal for a farmer. He has found a job on a boat, and Molly agrees to cook for him. Sam, the owner of the boat, then wins $5,000 in a lottery; and, in a sentimental gesture, he gives half the boat to Dan'l, if the young man will serve as the captain.

In the second scene, Molly and Dan'l are shown living happily—and chastely, we are made to believe—together. The first trouble in their Eden stems from a decision by the county-fair committee that Molly cannot compete in the cooking contests since she is not a permanent resident of the county. A lovers' quarrel develops when Molly decides that Dan'l is afraid of Klore, who has recently been released from jail for fighting. Dan'l, in truth, is unconcerned with Klore. Molly invites Klore aboard the boat; but Klore, already drunk, passes out, and no fight is possible. Dan'l leaves, but it is clear that he is concerned only with Molly, to whom he gives his share of the boat.

The last act returns the play to the opening scene, in Hennessey's Hotel in Rome, New York. It is November, the end of the canal boating season; and the time of year is symbolic of the future of the canal. It is dying. The railroads are spreading their influence. Molly now is to have a second chance to enter a cooking contest, this time at the State Fair. Klore has remained sober, preparing to fight Dan'l, who he believes had beaten him when he was drunk. Molly has refused Dan'l's gift of his share of the boat; and, although she loves him, she still feels she should be loyal to the canal.

The melodramatic action of the play reaches a climax with the arrival of Klore. Molly attempts to spare Dan'l a beating by pretending Dan'l is another man. He, however, refuses to hide, and defeats Klore with little effort. This conflict, it seems, was never a serious problem, and its solution—Dan'l's victory over Klore—is simply the means by which Molly may now become the "farmer's wife."

Although the victory of the railroad (progress) over the canal (the old Eden) is assured, Molly finds one way to avoid obvious surrender. "Are you goin' take a honeymoon trip on a train?" one of the characters, Solomon, asks her.

"No," she replies. "We're goin' to the farm in a horse and buggy."

But even with progress, it is suggested that humanism—the folk ways—will continue. The first act ended with the characters singing the Erie Canal song. Now, the play ends with "The Railroad Song." It is true, as Fortune verbalizes in the second act, that life on the canal is perfect: "It's all so perfect and everyone's so happy, you'd think nothing could lick it." But the nostalgia is conventional. Unlike *Rome Haul,* in *The Farmer Takes a Wife* the retreat to the farm, the end of the canal, the growth of the railroad are all a part of the "happy ending."

After the Broadway run of this play, *The Farmer Takes a Wife* was purchased by Hollywood and turned into a motion picture, with Henry Fonda re-creating the role of Dan'l, the part he had played on the stage. Connelly, who was then under contract to Warner Brothers to make a motion picture of *The Green Pastures,* aided in the translation of *The Farmer Takes a Wife* from stage play to screen play. In fact, for most of the 1930's and the early 1940's, Connelly made his home in Hollywood, keeping his New York apartment on Central Park West for frequent visits.

VII   *A Broadway Failure*

There were expectations during these years that a new stage play written by Connelly alone would soon be forthcoming. In late December, 1938, however, when he did make his return to the New York stage, there was a double disappointment. Again he was working in collaboration—this time with Arnold Sundgaard on a play called *Everywhere I Roam;* and the critics did not like the play.

There were kind words said about the production, which Connelly, himself, had done in collaboration with Bela Blau. *Time,* for example, conceded that "There are good folk-dancing and singing in *Everywhere I Roam* . . . and fine pictorial moments." "But the play itself," the *Time* critic judged, "is dull and its message is hopelessly sentimental and confused." It is essentially "the message," in fact, that *Time* attacked: "It is one thing to satirize the evils of predatory industrialism and hymn the praises of clean and sturdy toil. But it is nonsense to give the impression that hardship is better than ease . . . or that the profit motive was first discovered shortly before the Civil War."[27]

We might judge that the *Time* reviewer allowed the political bias of his journal to determine his critical judgment of the play; however, the general critical rejection of *Everywhere I Roam* was seemingly made purely on theatrical grounds. Even a sensitive, liberal critic like John Mason Brown, who probably shared most of Connelly's social views, was not pleased with *Everywhere I Roam.* He recognized that Connelly faced a number of problems that had nothing to do artistically with the play itself. In the first place, 1938–39 was a theatrical year, Mr.

Brown commented, in which the playwrights were attempting to be affirmative. "Like Mr. Rice and Mr. Sherwood and Mr. Anderson, the authors of 'Everywhere I Roam' have turned to the stage to have their affectionate say about these United States." The results of their intentions, according to Brown, are two acts that are "soft-headed and monotonous," presenting "the record of a century of retrogress told in satiric terms that are at once familiar and feeble. In chronicling this century Mr. Sundgaard and Mr. Connelly proved to be paradoxical playwrights. In their technique they are streamlined.... But in their thinking they insist upon riding up and down the Lincoln Highway with tears in their eyes (because it is no longer a bumpy road) and with a copy of Rousseau under their arms."[28] It was, it would seem, the failure to reconcile theatrical techniques with philosophical assumptions—rather than the assumptions themselves—that annoyed Mr. Brown.

Everywhere I Roam was, in one sense, Connelly's most serious failure on the stage. *The Deep Tangled Wildwood* may have gotten more hoots from the critics; *How's the King?* may have had scenery that fell; but *Everywhere I Roam* failed in spite of— or maybe because of—the care and concern given it. Mantle commented that "Connelly tried valiantly to do something with and for . . ." the play, and then he added, "it being Mr. Sundgaard's contention that he did altogether too much."[29] The play closed after thirteen performances, and Connelly never again collaborated with anyone on a stage play.

VIII *The Free Company Presents . . .*

Connelly, it seems clear, was still available for projects that he felt important. He turned down the offer to direct Nugent and Thurber's *Male Animal* in 1939 only because he thought the real subject of the play, academic freedom, had been obfuscated by lesser elements.[30] However, when James Boyd asked Connelly to do a radio play for a series "about the meaning of America," he responded immediately with his short drama, *The Mole on Lincoln's Cheek*.[31]

As Boyd comments about the response of writers to his request for scripts, "The demand for a piece of unpaid-for work in a medium [radio] unfamiliar to many of them was a serious one."

Connelly and the other playwrights who responded—Maxwell Anderson, Sherwood Anderson, Stephen Vincent Benet, Paul Green, Archibald MacLeish, William Saroyan, Robert Sherwood, and Orson Welles—knew they had nothing to gain financially or professionally from the experience. Connelly, it seems, considered this a worthwhile opportunity "to explain and illustrate [some facet of] the meaning of our freedom;"[32] and he took the subject that he thought Nugent and Thurber had neglected, academic freedom.

The Mole on Lincoln's Cheek was the second play performed in the series; and, as with so much of Connelly's work in the drama, professional theater people were impressed with Connelly's ability to use the stage imaginatively. As a play, *The Mole on Lincoln's Cheek* is a slight work, intentionally constructed so that it might be done by amateur groups. In writing of the plays in the series, however, S. M. Smith mentions *The Mole on Lincoln's Cheek* more than any other play presented, commenting upon its versatility for stage or radio, the skillful use of Impressionistic devices, and its generally successful use of theatrical effects.[33]

For *The Mole on Lincoln's Cheek,* Connelly returns to that small town "West of Pittsburgh," Millersville, the setting for *The Deep Tangled Wildwood;* but his concern is no longer with the old-fashioned ways but with the fundamental American character and intellectual honesty. The action concerns an investigation of a young teacher, Miss Thatcher, who is being examined for her "unpatriotic statements" about American heroes. She has commented, for example, that John Hancock, when he was not signing the Declaration of Independence, was a smuggler.

In a scene in which she faces her accusers—a member of the school board and the head of the Millersville Veterans' League—she is defended by her principal, the romantic interest in the play, and by the superintendent. It is the superintendent, Dr. Hunter, who speaks of the mole on Lincoln's cheek—to him a symbol that Americans want the truth, even about the "defects" of their heroes. The "other way" of education—that being followed in Nazi Germany—is set in contrast to Miss Thatcher's practice. The school board member is won over, but the veterans' organization man remains unconvinced. He is, however, outvoted. "We know that everything considered," the school board man says of the United States, "it's one of the best countries ever organized. And we want to keep it that way. And that means not being afraid to learn what made it tick in the beginning and what keeps it going."

IX   Land of the Living[34]

The Mole on Lincoln's Cheek was not, of course, the work that Connelly had been promising. Although the public did not see the promised work in the 1930's, Connelly had written it. In 1938, he copyrighted *The Land of the Living*, a three-act play. He made no effort, however, to have it produced at that time, but seemingly kept working on it. In 1952, he copyrighted a revised version of this play, titled *There Are Two Points;*[35] and six years later, on March 1, 1958, this play, now titled *Hunter's Moon,* was produced at the Winter Garden in London.[36]

Apparently Connelly had *Land of the Living* ready to start production when Sundgaard interested him in *Everywhere I Roam.* These two plays have much in common; and it is understandable, after the failure of *Everywhere I Roam,* that he postponed staging his own play. Connelly, seemingly, made an error in judgment in this decision, for, whatever else may be said of *Land of the Living,* it seems certain that it would have been more successful than *Everywhere I Roam.*

The basic theme of *Land of the Living*—that life should have meaning and quietude—is, as Connelly indicates in the text of the play itself, from Thoreau, not from the Progressive reform philosophy of the 1930's. It is a theme to which he returns—more happily, I think—in his novel, *A Souvenir from Qam,* in 1965; but the play, in spite of faults, is probably a superior work to *The Farmer Takes a Wife.*

One of Connelly's problems as a playwright has been that, even in the midst of his most serious moments, there is the temptation to solve the tragic with Algonquin wit. As a romantic intellectual, Connelly seems to find it difficult to see any condition as being beyond the control of the mind and good intentions of man. In the midst of *The Land of the Living*—a work to which Connelly obviously gave a great deal of attention—we find echoes of *The Deep Tangled Wildwood.* In the search of

David Rudderman, the protagonist of the play, for a life of meaning, we sometimes encounter the mind of the Broadway wit of the 1920's seeking an adjustment.

The first scene of the play is largely a discussion of what a life of meaning should be. David, who has just inherited about twenty million dollars and a large section of the Adirondack Mountains, has been a history professor at an Iowa college. He now plans to retire to his mountain estate, marry Ann Tabor, and live the life of Henry Thoreau. Walden for David, a specialist in Colonial American history, is to be, however, not an observation of wild life about him, but a contemplation of the past.

The contrast between the modern age and the Eden of the past is established in a dialogue between David and Kit, an old mountain guide. Kit is becoming corrupted by modern life, listening to the radio and having "no time" to read, being more concerned with the question of the facts of commercials than the truths of nature. He does still recognize that the past (an age in which towns were named for qualities of the spirit—"Serenity," "Perseverance," "Industry"—"Kinda like mottoes") had its values; but it is David, not Kit, who yearns for an age when men chose serenity rather than excitement, perseverance rather than ease, and industry rather than comfort. Like his ancestor of eight generations ago, Isaiah, who found a wife, Martha, in Serenity and saved her when the village was destroyed, David yearns for adventures of the spirit.

In the second scene of the first act, David returns to a New England village of the past. As this scene opens, it appears for a moment that this play will imitate the return-to-the-past device of *Berkeley Square,* a play Connelly admired when he directed it in 1930. The stage directions, in fact, describe the scene as "the Colonial village of Serenity in 1750." The townspeople are preparing a festival, a pageant to celebrate the founding of the town; and the importance which the play gives to this pageant makes it clear that the scene is intended to suggest what meaningful drama should be—an enactment of one's personal history. Underlying the general theatrical excitement is a current of anxiety concerning the return of the leader, who is at the moment away from the town-fort making a peace treaty with the Indians, and this concern strengthens the suggestion that the play is a flashback in time.

During the rehearsal, a plane flies overhead; and a few minutes later, David enters, seemingly a time-machine visitor. There has, however, been no voyage through time. The village of Serenity, in spite of its costumes, speech, and setting, really does exist in the twentieth century; but it has been kept purposely isolated from the rest of civilization to preserve its virtue, its "serenity." In fact, it exists on a plot of land owned by David and marked "off limits" as a "Wild Life Preserve." In Serenity, David meets Cynthia Abernathy—a descendant of the same Martha Abernathy who had met and married David's ancestor eight generations earlier. David and Cynthia fall in love at first sight.

David intends to remain in Serenity; but, as the second act develops, he is made aware that he is not welcome. The two "inhabitants" of Serenity who are cognizant of the outside world see in him a danger to the virtue of this private world. David tells one of them, Roger, that he does not wish to remain in the modern world, that he renounces it. In Serenity, he argues, he has found "... the heart and spirit of a world that is still young." Roger tells him that all men are sick of the present and long for the past, but a man must live in his own age. If David tries to become a part of Serenity, he will only destroy it. Since David has an obligation to return to the modern world to break his engagement to Ann, he is willing to leave temporarily; but, to force them to accept him upon his return, he agrees with Cynthia's suggestion that she accompany him. The village, he thinks, will have to accept them if they are together.

In the last act, David and Cynthia return to the outside world, on the eve of David's scheduled wedding day. Cynthia is shocked by the outside world, terrified by such mechanical "monsters" as an electric organ, which causes her to faint. Connelly here does not satirize modern life. It is not the evil of modern life—the unemployment, the confusion, the crime, the slums, the violence—that frightens Cynthia, but merely the tempo and values as these are symbolized by modern mechanics. When she recovers, Roger comes to her, tells her she has been dreaming, and leads her back to Serenity. David and Ann pursue them, but Serenity and Cynthia are, forever, lost to him. Ann, he realizes, must be his Cynthia; and he must find his own "Serenity" in his own time.

Critics concerned with social criticism will be as little pleased with *The Land of the Living* as they were with the "social philosophy" of *The Wisdom Tooth.* Cynthia, in terms of realistic, psychological drama, is not convincing. All of the people she meets in her short visit to the outside world are kind, almost impossibly considerate and self-sacrificing; and the scene is pleasant and rural. If she faints in this setting, what would she do in the face of the German buzz-bombs that were soon to be turning London into a nightmare, or at the sight of New York slums or of concentration camps? Connelly is, however, not concerned with the *objects* that shock one, but with the qualities. Cynthia is a citizen of the village of Serenity; and, even in a world of decent, kind people, serenity has been destroyed in the modern age.

Although my discussion of Connelly's career in the 1930's ends with a play that has never been published nor even produced in its original form, I do not intend to suggest that the "fresh woods" beyond the green pastures turned out to be barren fields. There is, to be sure, no single piece of work in this period that equals *Merton of the Movies* or *The Wisdom Tooth,* let alone *The Green Pastures;* but Connelly was not in retirement. *The Land of the Living,* in spite of its present neglect, is a work of much merit and of some importance in understanding his total view; and *The Farmer Takes a Wife* yet remains an accomplishment in the sentimental comedy. As far as published works are concerned, this period is one of the least productive of Connelly's career; but, if he had been more zealous about his literary reputation, he would not have been the kind of man who could have written *The Green Pastures.* His failures in this period—working with *Everywhere I Roam,* neglecting his own work to help others with theirs—were professional miscalculations to be lamented by the literary critic; but they do not detract from the quality of the man.

CHAPTER 6

A Time to Start Again

LATE in 1941, Connelly returned to Broadway, bringing with him a new play, *The Flowers of Virtue*, the first full-length play for the stage that he had written alone since *The Green Pastures,* and the first major play entirely of his own conception that he had staged since *The Wisdom Tooth.* In spite of the failure of *Everywhere I Roam* and Connelly's long absence as a New York playwright, his name was still an exciting one on Broadway; and, even if Broadway audiences had not approved a Connelly play since *The Farmer Takes a Wife,* his work with other plays, as a director and producer, had earned him critical respect. Two of the plays with which he had worked—Eleanor and Herbert Farjeon's *Two Bouquets,* which he staged at the Windsor Theatre in 1938,[1] and Charlotte Armstrong's *Happiest Days,* which he staged in 1939[3]—had both received favorable reviews.

Connelly's production of *The Flowers of Virtue* in 1942 seemed, therefore, for many in the theater not so much a new start as it did "business as usual." His work as a director, producer, collaborator, screen writer, and general promotion man, however—no matter how well he had been rewarded for it financially[3]—had always seemed of minor importance in comparison to his dramatic writing; and it was as a playwright that Connelly was being "welcomed home." One newspaper, in reporting that *The Flowers of Virtue* had been announced, commented that *The Green Pastures* ". . . alone would make him a sure candidate for the theatrical history books. And when you add to this 20 years of writing and directing some of our best-loved comedies, you can understand why the first hints there may be a new Connelly play in the offing set up a slight attack of dancing in the streets on the part of the townspeople." Although attention was given by the reporter to Connelly's work as a director and producer, specifically mentioning *Having Wonderful Time,* and to his screen writing in Hollywood, the primary emphasis was given to his plays—*Dulcy, Merton of the Movies, To the Ladies!, Beggar on Horseback, The Wisdom Tooth, The Green Pastures,* and *The Farmer Takes a Wife.*[4] These seven works were in 1942, and are now the basis of his reputation as a dramatist; and it was as the author of these that Marc Connelly was being cheered. New York theater-goers hoped that *The Flowers of Virtue* would be added to the list.

Connelly seems to have worked on the new play for several years before bringing it to New York, and he had spent some of his time as a Hollywood resident in researching the locale for the play, Mexico. "This is a good time to record," a New York reporter wrote, "that Connelly becomes an expert on any play that he writes." Following a summary of the research that the playwright had done for *The Green Pastures* and for *The Farmer Takes a Wife,* the reporter then told his readers of the exact care that Connelly had taken with *The Flowers of Virtue:* "The Mexican furniture, ornaments, hangings, and so forth are authentic. . . ."[5]

By 1942 the New York theater was in need of new plays. The war years were, as Robert Warnock has noted, good years for commercial theater: "The general economic inflation in America during the war years and the sudden prosperity of those who stayed at home were reflected in the short-lived [1941–45] boom in the theatre."[6] Old theater-goers had more money for entertainment, and they were being joined by a new breed—young servicemen on leave, war workers, migrants to the big cities. It was a good time to start again.

I   *The Failure*

War years are a good time for daring, for the spectacular, for the bold push, for the untempered statement; and the World War II years, especially in the first months when the outcome of the war was still uncertain, were no time for moderation. Connelly, however, as befits one who twice backed Adlai Stevenson for the Presidency, has always been a moderate man, one who believes in qualifications. Most of the critics recognized that *The Flowers of Virtue* had, as Burns Mantle phrased it, "an exalted purpose"; but, like Mantle, they complained that Connelly's approach was "timid and the result disappointing and regrettable."[7]

The play ran only three nights, opening February 5, 1942, and closing February 7.[8] The critics were not pleased. Rosamond Gilder called it "a mild and didactic script."[9] George Freedley, praising Connelly's directing, casting, and staging, acknowledged that the play "has many bright, humorous spots"; but he concluded that "... it fails to advance a single, sound dramatic idea. There are individual scenes of great merit, but the play as a whole adds up to nothing which thrills you in the theatre." The problem with *The Flowers of Virtue,* as Mr. Freedley saw it then, was that it "... had some of the simplicity of a parable without the vitality of a great message to impart."[10]

Frank Farrell also complained of the lack of force of the play. "Somebody must have pointed out to Marc Connelly that the trouble with most anti-Nazi plays is that they are about as subtle as a pair of club feet in approaching their point.... So Mr. Connelly finally got around to writing *The Flowers of Virtue,* a comedy so flimsy in texture that the author has left himself no leg at all, on which to stand. . . . *The Flowers of Virtue,*" he concluded his review, "might have been received more graciously six years ago, but I doubt it. It doesn't hurt Hitler ten per cent as much as it will Howard Cullman and Mrs. Marshall Field, the backers."[11] Farrell obviously believed Connelly had tried to write a propaganda play, and failed.

Despite the wartime boom in theater, it should be pointed out, war plays in general did not do well in New York during 1941–42, a fact that more than one reviewer noted even at the time. Freedley, for example, began his review of *The Flowers of Virtue* by commenting that "... the season of 1941–42 will go down in theatrical history as the year in which the major playwrights had nothing to say to their audience."[12] All of the plays he listed to prove his point were "war plays" of one sort or another by such people as Maxwell Anderson, Charles MacArthur, George S. Kaufman, Edna Ferber, and John Steinbeck. Mantle, too, in making the same observation, added another reason for the fail-

ure of such plays as George Kaufman and Edna Ferber's *The
Land Is Bright,* Norman Krasna's *The Man with Blond Hair,*
and John Steinbeck's *The Moon Is Down.* They failed, Mantle
argued, because they "asked sympathy for a representative of the
enemy."[13]

Considering the unanimous disapproval of *The Flowers of
Virtue* by the theater reviewers, the biographer of Connelly
might do well to pass over this play with the simple report of its
New York failure. Connelly, himself, has never defended the
play; and, since he has not arranged for publication during the
twenty-five years that have passed since its production,[14] we
might assume that he accepts the critical response of 1942. Moreover, since, according to the critics of 1942, the play was intended as a "parable" of the rise and fall of Nazism, aimed to
"hurt" Hitler, it does not seem likely that it would find a more
sympathetic audience now.

II   *The Play*

The Flowers of Virtue,[15] despite the general critical opinion,
is not a propaganda play. It is anti-authoritarian, and it does
have an historical relationship to the rise of dictatorships. The
play, however, is concerned with politics only as a background
for the real subject—man's need to affirm his humanism in the
midst of any kind of tyranny. *The Flowers of Virtue* is, moreover, probably as carefully wrought as any play Connelly has
ever written; but there were problems with the last bits of its
composition. Although the play opened six weeks after the
United States entered the war, Connelly had completed it sometime before December 7, 1941. In fact, the outbreak of the war
caused him to add a bit about the effects of Pearl Harbor on
Mexican neutrality, especially in relationship to Germany. The
play, for example, is set on December 7, 1941, the day the Japanese attacked Pearl Harbor. These last-minute changes—however necessary they may have been for any war play opening in
those first weeks after war was declared—add nothing to the
work. Indeed, Mr. Connelly told me that he knows now that he
should have withdrawn the work when war was declared.

The Flowers of Virtue, it should be repeated, is not primarily
an anti-Nazi play; rather it is a play—like *The Wisdom Tooth*—

that is concerned with a man's loss of courage and purpose. Like *The Wisdom Tooth,* this play also has a protagonist named Bemis; and the Grover Bemis of *The Flowers of Virtue* could almost be the Charley Bemis of *The Wisdom Tooth*—twenty years older and again in need of help. Like Charley, Grover has lost his integrity; and, like Charley, Grover regains a purpose in life through association with youth. Nancy, Grover's daughter, serves the same function in this play that Skeeter serves in *The Wisdom Tooth.*

The Flowers of Virtue does have political overtones. The would-be Hitler of Mexico, General Orijas, however, patterns his rise to power, not on the career of the German dictator, but on that of Charley's old political target, Coolidge. The Germans, the Italians, and even, in one instance, the Russians are viewed as "the enemy" of freedom and honesty; but nowhere is the indictment of totalitarian methods so strong as it was even in *The Mole on Lincoln's Cheek.* In part, Connelly is still playing the Algonquin wit with his political material. General Orijas, who plans to take over the Mexican government and return it to "a feudal system," has an even wilder scheme in mind when he achieves power. He will "Get Warner Broothers to make a life of Presidente Co-oolidge, with George Raft" playing the President. Nancy avoids dinner with Carlota Garcia, the ex-American novelist, because Carlota left the United States, announcing that she had "... lost confidence in a country that hung on to Roosevelt." Obviously, by Nancy's standards—and Connelly's—anyone that anti-Roosevelt must be unpatriotic.

The political comments, however, are merely trappings. The play is not primarily concerned with saving the world from dictatorship; instead, its concern is with the salvation of Grover Bemis, who is ill in mind, body, and soul. His illness, Nancy tells her mother, is spiritual. "In spite of all the years that people have spent trying to make him smug and self-satisfied, everything that was fine was trying to free itself," and this internal struggle is his illness.

Like Charley Bemis, Grover first attempts to "free" the decency in himself with futile efforts. He enlists for ambulance service in China, evidence for Mrs. Bemis that her husband has lost his mind. It is significant, I think, that Connelly, in 1941, picked Asia as the arena of Grover's service rather than Europe.

If the play were simply a tract against dictatorship, service in Europe should have been Grover's choice; but the play is less concerned with stopping the villains than in aiding the decent, the hungry, and the helpless. Asia with its millions of war-frightened, hungry people was an ideal place in 1942 for a man who wanted to free himself from the disease of smugness and self-satisfaction through service to others.

In the course of the three acts of *The Flowers of Virtue,* Grover, who is in Mexico to escape responsibility, discovers that his services are still needed, that he is still of value to people trying to create a "better" life. In the Mexican pueblo, *Las Flores de la Virtud* (the Flowers of Virtue), Grover sees a decent, progressive man—Trinidad Perez—about to be destroyed by Orijas and Carlota because he stands in the way of their plans for wealth, power, and reactionary grandeur. Neither Perez nor Bemis, for that matter, is really opposed to Orijas; rather, they are simply for progress. Perez, for example, attempts to establish a school; but the entire notion of practical education is offensive to Carlota. Although she has made her fortune turning out trashy, pretentious novels, she sees no need for the Mexican children to learn to read and write. "They," she says of the children, "learn their legends and handicrafts empirically"; and, in her opinion, this education is all they need.

Bemis is, in part, amused at the bumbling villainy of Orijas and his chief lieutenant, Ezequiel. Orijas' plan to create a strike and then end it by executing Perez—a plan worked out in the belief that he is imitating what ". . . Calveen Co-oolidge deed in the State of Massa-chu-*setts*"—amuses Bemis, who pretends to agree with Orijas that Coolidge had Harding killed as his means to power. Then, too, none of the villains is really punished, although Orijas is forced to flee from the Federal authorities.

What Bemis discovers—"in a miracle"—is not how to stop a Hitler but how to keep from being a "Babbitt." He tells his daughter, ". . . there *are* things to believe in, things to fight for, and that's all *anyone* needs to make life exciting and good." Bemis also discovers that the good life of the future is not only for the young, but for anyone who is willing to use what he knows to aid human decency. Frank Farrell was probably right in complaining that *The Flowers of Virtue* was "out of step with the times.''[16] For a play about love and private decency, 1942 was not a good year.

III   *The Lights Dim*

With the failure of *The Flowers of Virtue,* Connelly made no more overtures to New York as a playwright for the duration of the war. There is no reason to suppose that he was disappointed with either himself or with Broadway. Although Connelly has always felt that the critics, generally speaking, do not understand the stage, he has never once blamed them for a failure. As a matter of fact, during these war years, he was at work on another play; he was still searching for "a new Richard B. Harrison"; and he was enjoying "himself particularly in 'Our Town'."[17] The promised play was not finished; the new Harrison was not found; but Connelly added a little to his legend with his enactment of the role of the Stage Manager in *Our Town.*

Connelly, as the Stage Manager, according to John Chapman, was "something of a treasure. His ease and ability are in excellent keeping with the role."[18] After a three-week run during which he won the applause and the gratitude of all associated with the production, Marc Connelly announced, in Mr. Mercer fashion, his "retirement" from acting, suggesting at the same time that should the "part be right," he might again be available for other roles. The announcement was made in the spirit of the Algonquin wits, but back of the tongue-in-cheek phrases, there was a genuine note of nostalgia and fatigue. He told a reporter that his failure to have a new play produced in recent seasons did not mean that he had lost interest in the stage. Connelly, according to a reporter at the time, "has many plans and projects for 1944. He is willing to leave acting to òthers for awhile. But he wants to produce a play or two—and finish writing one. He will get in some work in Hollywood, where he is one of the highest paid writers. He will continue his quest for ... a successor to Richard B. Harrison."[19]

His return as a major playwright with *The Flowers of Virtue* had not been successful, and Connelly knew that the old world—the world in which he had made his reputation as a playwright —was dying. In commenting on one of the plays he had seen in the 1940's, John Van Druten's *Voice of the Turtle*, Connelly noted, "That girl and that soldier suggest the uprooting of humanity that we're witnessing in the world right now." He had thought that *The Flowers of Virtue* had also said something about the subject, but New York theater-goers had not responded. Either his concept of humanism—expressed by the positive, if small, constructive act of the single individual—was out of fashion, or he had lost the ability to communicate his view. Perhaps no one remembered "Calveen Co-oolidge" any more.

Connelly was fifty-five years old when the war ended. He had not had a Broadway success with one of his own plays in almost a dozen years, but he was financially secure, and he still had a reputation as a New York playwright and Hollywood screen writer. His successes had stayed fresh; his failures—with the odd exception of *The Deep Tangled Wildwood*—were quickly forgotten by the stage historians and critics. It must have seemed like a good time to make a graceful exit. Without ever really saying "Good-by," Marc Connelly in the mid-years of the 1940's changed from an "active" playwright of the American theater to an elder statesman of letters, a man now able to sit back and contemplate the scene. This change, as Connelly's work during the past twenty years gives ample evidence, was not really a matter of a decrease in activity but a change in attitude. There were still things to do, but *The Flowers of Virtue* appears to be the last work intended as an accomplishment to set people "dancing in the streets."

In his reminiscent essays of the last fifteen years, Connelly has returned on various occasions to the McKeesport of his youth, to the New York of the 1920's, to the Hollywood during his days of glory filming *The Green Pastures*. Only once, to my knowledge, has he returned to the war years; and the episode he selected, the death of his friend Robert Benchley, is symbolic for this period. Connelly wrote that when he heard of Benchley's death late in 1945,

> Suddenly the world seemed a duller place....
> Somebody recalled what Robert had said after George Ade's death: "When a great humorist dies, everyone should go to a place where there is laughter, and drink to his memory until the lights go out."
> Those of us who loved Robert decided to do exactly that. Groups

gathered at two restaurants he was devoted to, 21 in New York and Romanoff's in Beverly Hills. We reminisced about him and the funny things he said and did. . . . Finally it was time to go home. The lights had gone out.[20]

CHAPTER 7

An Elder Statesman of Letters

IT IS A RARE STUDY of American drama between the two world wars that is without some account of Marc Connelly; it is an equally rare study of American drama since 1945 that mentions him. The first circumstance is easier to understand than the second, if we compare Connelly's work of the past twenty years with his work during the two decades of his greatest successes at least as far as quantity is concerned.

There is something absurd about the willingness of contemporary theater to allow new plays by men like Connelly, Thornton Wilder, and William Saroyan to pass almost unobserved. American drama is not rich enough to afford such waste, and it has caused a rupture between the theater before and after World War II that reminds one of the break in the English drama between the Restoration and the eighteenth century. With the exceptions of Eugene O'Neill and Lillian Hellman, no American playwright who reached prominence before Pearl Harbor is now given much serious attention, especially for works done after the war. As far as Marc Connelly is concerned, it is generally assumed that, if he did not stop writing for the stage with *The Green Pastures* or *The Farmer Takes a Wife,* he most assuredly did after *The Flowers of Virtue.*

That part of the American public interested in theater, literature, and the arts in general has, of course, been aware that Connelly is often in the news for his support of this-or-that cause dear to the hearts of literate people; however, the notion that he is an active force in drama, the way Albee and Miller, for example, are, is held by no one. It is true that most people aware of him are pleased with him. He stands for the right causes; he is charming and witty and a gentleman—generous with his time and talent; forthright, yet tolerant; a sane voice in a mad-mad world; a gentle quip in a world of anger.

Critics and theater historians today think of Connelly much as the eighteenth-century critics thought of William Congreve during the first quarter of that century, after *The Way of the World*. The comparison is not altogether unfair. Both men turned out a number of superb comedies; both achieved "greatness" with a single work; both *seemed* to remain *around* the theater, but not *in* it. From the point of view of the academic critic, concerned only with plays that were critically or financially successful, the comparison seems apt. *The Green Pastures* was, as far as popular and critical reputation is concerned, Connelly's *Way of the World*.

A review of Mr. Connelly's "achievements" since the end of World War II does not challenge such a view. Connelly has not had a single successful new play produced or published. There has been no edition of his "complete works" and no major revivals, except for one of *The Green Pastures,* of his plays in the theater. He has not yet completed his long-awaited "memoirs." In fact, with the exception of *A Souvenir from Qam* and some short sketches and travel articles, none of Connelly's works of the past twenty years is generally available for critical examination.

In spite of this lack of a "public record," however, Mr. Connelly is not a modern Congreve in retirement. In the last twenty years, he has had three "new" full-length plays produced on the professional stage: *A Story for Strangers* (1948); *There Are Two Points* (a revision of *Land of the Living*) copyrighted in 1952 and later staged as *Hunter's Moon* (1958); and *The Portable Yenberry* (1962). Mr. Connelly has also continued to work with the theater in such enterprises as his and Jean Dalrymple's production of *Hope for the Best* (1945);[1] his staging of his own play, *A Story for Strangers* (1948); his full-scale revival of *The Green Pastures* (1951);[2] his direction and production of *Hunter's Moon* on the London stage (1958);[3] and his production of *The Portable Yenberry* for Purdue University (1962).

He has been active in a variety of projects, political and theatrical. He was a Commissioner for dramatic arts for the United Nations. He served with the late Mrs. Franklin D. Roosevelt as chairman of the New York State Volunteers for Stevenson in 1956. He and Thornton Wilder were advisors for the Equity Theatre Library, created to honor his old friend, F. P. Adams. He was a commentator for the national networks for the Republican Presidential Convention in 1964.

In spite of the fact that he announced his retirement from acting in 1944, after *Our Town,* he has, during the past twenty years, done enough acting so that he now has an impressive reputation as a character actor. He returned to the stage in 1946 as the Stage Manager in a London production of *Our Town,* was a substitute disc-jockey for the late Ernie Kovacs, made guest appearances on the Jack Paar show, played a supporting role in a television drama series, *The Defenders,*[4] and played one of the leading character roles in both the stage and screen versions of *Tall Story* in 1959. Early in 1967, he had a supporting role in the television drama, *The Borgia Stick.*

During the past twenty years, too, he has been established as one of the "elder statesmen of letters." For almost five years, from 1947 to 1952, he was a professor of playwriting at Yale University; and in 1953 he was elected president of the National Institute of Arts and Letters.

It would be an easy matter to justify a public interest in Connelly for his general contributions to civilized well-being—because a play is better for his presence, a television program more entertaining, a political convention less pompous, a magazine more readable; and indeed newspaper reviewers, theater directors, and the general public do treasure this public Marc Connelly. He is again and again called "the Winston Churchill of American humor," the "dewdrop man," the "erudite" Mr. Connelly, the "puckish" Mr. Connelly. Everyone likes him; everyone admires him, even the same critics and reviewers who are either unaware that he is also an active man of letters, or, when aware, wish that they were not.

It is, however, our task to move from the man and evaluate the work, to make some sort of judgment as to whether his recent plays, his novel, his sketches belong to the ages or to the waste basket. It is my private judgment that, if Connelly merits recognition for *Dulcy, The Wisdom Tooth,* and *The Farmer Takes a Wife*—that if these plays have qualities that readers and playgoers want to keep alive—there is a serious oversight in the failure to add *A Story for Strangers, There Are Two Points,* and *The Portable Yenberry* to the Connelly library of available works.

In summarizing the state of American drama in 1965, Allan Lewis saw "healthy indications ... of a return to an affirmation of life and to the search for positive belief." In Professor Lewis' opinion, "Total negativism may have run its course."[5] If it has, it ran its course without any help from Marc Connelly. It is, in fact, appropriate that Connelly should have staged *Hope for the Best* in 1945, at the very time that American dramatists were turning to "despair" as the only respectable condition for adult drama. The title fits Connelly's general attitude toward life, especially as it is reflected in his three plays of this period: *A Story for Strangers, There Are Two Points,* and *The Portable Yenberry.* None of these plays has been, thus far, successful on stage, and none has been published; but, if Professor Lewis is right, and if the "new" drama is returning "to an affirmation of life and to the search for positive belief," Connelly's plays may be back in style.

I   A Story for Strangers[6]

In May, 1947, when Connelly was appointed to the faculty of Yale University, *Time* summarized his career after *The Green Pastures:* "He has never risen to such heights again—he has spent his time writing or directing a couple of minor successes and a couple of major turkeys, acting a bit, devising Hollywood dialogue, and 'heading too many committees'."[7] At that time Connelly was at work on a new play, *A Story for Strangers,* which opened in October, 1948. The play—written by Connelly alone and directed by him—has a number of features that should have made it of special interest to those who characterized *The Green Pastures* as "such heights," for it resembles that work in its intent. *Time,* however, did not see it as a return to the "heights," but as one more "major turkey." "*A Story for Strangers,*" *Time* reported, "... is told, *via* flashbacks, to a traveling salesman in a small-town barbershop, and is quite as dull, and ten times as long, as the usual barber's yarn. . . . The play, a kind of *Passing of the Third Feedbox Back,* died at the end of the week."[8]

Joseph Wood Krutch commented that the play was so bad that he would not have reviewed it at all if it had not been written by a playwright of Connelly's stature. Krutch objected to Connelly's subject—the reformation of a town through "the Golden Rule." "... I doubt that this tale [any "Golden Rule" reform story, which he finds generally a poor tale] has ever been worse told than in 'A Story for Strangers' ...," he wrote. He did acknowledge that "I do not think I ever met a version [of the Golden Rule tale] which really came off," but *A Story for Strangers* was, in his judgment, utterly without merit. "Everything," he wrote, "except possibly the intention, is wrong, beginning with the fable."[9]

By Krutch's account, the play "... concerns a nice young man who wins his girl while he is living in an abandoned stable with an aged horse he has befriended. When the counterman from a hamburger stand invokes the Roman goddess of the stables, the horse is transformed and begins to harangue the leading citizens of the community. ... The equine discourse is inaudible to those in the paying audience, but is apparently concerned with the errors of the human race, and it is so effective that the village chippy turns chaste, the dairy owner begins leaving free milk to the needy, and the banker cancels mortgages right and left." Even the structure of the play—". . . a series of awkwardly managed flashbacks"—is too poor to deserve analysis. "Mr. Connelly," Krutch continues, "appears to go on the assumption that there are only two styles, the one which is realistic and the one which isn't." He concludes, "While we are about it, we might add that the direction is equally inept."

Mr. Krutch's review is typical of the critical response to *A Story for Strangers.* Writing under the name, "Kappo Phelan," the reviewer for *Commonweal* called his comments "... a non-review of a non-play. ..." He was amused by what he considered Mr. Connelly's philosophical stumbling. "Mr. Connelly ... wanted a Hero and he chose a Horse. I suppose the philosophy of the play could be called horse-sense. ..."[10]

Wolcott Gibbs dismissed even the intention of the play: "Another substandard miracle which resolves everybody's difficulties .... This time it takes the form of a horse that talks, or at least is said to talk, since he is inaudible to the audience and visible only as a rosy glow offstage." Gibbs found the miracle "unrealistic." "This community ... is corrupt beyond your gaudiest dreams . . . the banker . . . and the chief of police are crooks, guilty of such crimes as selling automobiles for two thousand dollars over the list price, certainly a triumph of evil in 1934. . . ." Like Krutch, Gibbs, too, complained of the direction.[11]

It is difficult to judge a performance of a play from the script alone. It is clear enough that the critics did not like the play and that the audiences did not support it; but it is well to remember that reviewers' judgments and audience response do not always give any real indication of the nature or worth of a play. Within a few years after the failure of *A Story for Strangers,* a full-scale revival of *The Green Pastures* failed with the same audience.

As I have previously noted, *A Story for Strangers* has much in common with *The Green Pastures*—a likeness that must be more apparent in the reading than in the stage presentations, for not a single reviewer commented upon the similarity. Both plays are divided into two parts, with a number of scenes in each part. Both are a staging of a "narrative" that is concerned with something that demonstrates—in Connelly's terms—the "history of man." Both use folk materials and legends—those of the Romans, with New Testament overtones, in *A Story for Strangers*—to show an adventure among an American folk group: Midwestern white Americans in this play rather than the Southern Negroes of *The Green Pastures*. Both plays suggest that there is something miraculous in the quality of mercy.

Connelly's intentions in the staging of *A Story for Strangers* might not have been clear. The complaints of the critics show a confusion both in the mechanics of the staging and in the play itself, and perhaps the first led the critics to a confusion about the latter. Connelly, to be sure, has not labeled his characters "folk"; he did not announce—as he did in *The Green Pastures*— that he was retelling an ancient story in terms of the beliefs of the folk. It is possible, moreover, that his purpose in *A Story for Strangers* is clear only if we come to it in the context of Connelly's other works. If so, the failure of the play was a theatrical failure well deserved; but, next only to *The Green Pastures, A Story for Strangers* is Connelly's most complete statement about man's search for "paradise."

Paradise, for Connelly, is always a place of decency, of civilized consideration, of rational understanding. He is concerned in this play with the means by which a society—that of Huntsville, Michigan, in 1934—is reformed from a vicious town into a paradise of virtue. Gibbs was amused by Connelly's view of evil—overpriced automobiles; however, as in *The Green Pastures*, Connelly selects his episodes in *A Story for Strangers* from modern incidents, but the "evil" they represent has Biblical authority. Krutch, for example, finds the evidence of reform to be trivial— "the village chippy turns chaste"; but it should be noted that Audrey, the village prostitute turned manicurist by the change, is not really one of the reformed characters. Rather, like Mary Magdalen in the New Testament, Audrey is able to live a different outward life because she has been influenced by a good man. In the new society created by the miracle, she has a more respectable outlet for her decent nature. The banker's reformation may be startling to those who know small-town bankers; but Connelly is again drawing the idea from the New Testament—the character of the tax collector—and fitting it to the American character. The most serious crime is not—as Gibbs suggests—a kind of incredible dishonesty; it is rather a hardness of the heart that shows itself in the mean, petty, brutal acts of aggression that each member of the society performs against his neighbors.

Connelly, to be sure, is optimistic about the changes that would result should men, through knowledge, come to realize that morality leads not only to better people but also to a better society; Huntsville, it is made quite clear, is a miserable place in which to live before the change, even for those who are successful in their crimes. He does not, however, expect others to share his optimism.

The character Mercer, this time as a travelling salesman, is used in this play to represent the audience. He is, at first, fearful of the kind of place that Huntsville has been. He is there only by mistake, for he had thought the bus driver had said "Blountsville." Huntsville has had such a bad reputation that all salesmen avoid it. He is, moreover, suspicious of the kind of town that Huntsville has become, for he is suspicious of all miracles. Mercer is the stranger to whom the story is told; and, after he hears it, he says, ". . . it's the kind of thing you can't digest all at once." Newt Fender, the town barber, and Audrey are not offended by his disbelief. They know that they must tell the story to keep alive their own knowledge. "Wouldn't it be terrible," Newt asks Audrey, "if some day we began to doubt this one [miracle] ourselves?"

The sins and misery of Huntsville in 1934 are the "evils" of the depression Midwest; and Connelly indicates clearly the source of these evils—a loss of human knowledge that life was meant to be good for man. This belief may be less popular than the thesis he used for *The Green Pastures*—that man was meant to suffer; but Connelly is writing about a different folk with a different history. The American in 1930, when *The Green Pastures* was being produced, knew from firsthand experience that man's lot in life was to suffer; and, in Connelly's terms, such an American as his leading actor in that play, Richard B. Harrison, had grown to greatness through that knowledge. The white American of 1948, when *A Story for Strangers* was staged, was discovering the affluent society; and, in Connelly's terms, he needed to know that this affluence must rest on the common realization that there is enough to go around and more to share. "Virtue will return," Irving the horse tells the townspeople, "when you rid yourself of the fears that keep you from your inheritance." Man's inheritance, in the terms of this play, includes physical plenty and a society based upon concern for others and governed by rational men of good will.

A Story for Strangers probably would have succeeded better in the early 1930's when Franklin Roosevelt was speaking of the need for confidence and trust; but it was not until 1948, when the various welfare programs, with which Connelly had long been in sympathy, had demonstrated the thesis that people who give more have more, that the evidence was available. Connelly is not writing of a miracle that was to happen, but of one that had happened. And in Newt's terms, the danger was not that strangers would not believe the miracle, but rather that those who had participated in it—the Midwesterners now recovered from the depression—would forget it and again lose their inheritance.

A Story for Strangers may, as the critics complained, have been a "dull," misdirected play in performance; it is not, however, merely a boy-wins-girl sentimental comedy with a talking horse for a "hero."

II   There Are Two Points[12]

Connelly's second play for this period, *There Are Two Points,* needs but little additional discussion. In plot, structure, and theme it is still *The Land of the Living,* the play he copyrighted in 1938. The changes that Connelly made between the first version and the one he copyrighted in 1952 and then produced in 1958 in London[13] under the title *Hunter's Moon* have little purpose other than to update the play.

The first scene, in the second version, introduces David Rudderman's need for "Serenity" in terms other than those Connelly used in the 1930's. In the 1938 version, David had gone to the Rudderman estate, which he had inherited unexpectedly through the accidental death of his relatives, already discouraged with the failure of the machine age to solve the problems of modern life. He was "depression weary." In the second version, David is reasonably happy as a history professor; but he has been forced to take over management of the Rudderman estate because he is naturally the most capable. He is unhappy only because, as his fiancée Ann says, he is "forcing himself to be a tycoon." According to Ann, ". . . he loves his work back at the university, but his sense of duty won't let him admit it."

Connelly includes some of the narrative content of the 1938 script in the second version with a dialogue between David and his brother, Richard; but in many respects only superficial attention is paid to the Thoreau ideal of the simple life. In fact, all mentions of Thoreau in the first version are dropped in *There Are Two Points.* David becomes excited about "Serenity" and the past only when he is given a bundle of journals, written in the years between 1739 and 1753—journals that "could be a history of Serenity from its settlement to the day it was wiped out." David's interest, moreover, is professional; the journals are, in historical terms, "a valuable document."

The complaint of the London *Observer*[14] that it is never quite clear how David arrives in Serenity is, at least in terms of the typed script, not justified. David explains that his plane was forced down, and he wandered in. There is, however, a basic confusion in motivation that is probably reflected in the irritation of the *Observer* critic. The first scene of the 1938 script demonstrates David's weariness with the modern world in a dialogue with Kit, but Kit is dropped from the second version, and with him Connelly also dropped David's philosophical and emotional interest in an escape to a simpler age.

In the revised script, in the place of the first scene with its suggestions of the creeping decay of the mechanical age, is a scene set in the children's playhouse; and, except for David's desire to be a successful historian rather than a successful tycoon, he seems perfectly happy. Thus his speeches in the second scene of the First Act and in the Second Act, all retained without change from the 1938 version, are not logically motivated. The outside world may have been in trouble in 1952, as well as in 1938; but in the 1952 version, the audience would have no way of knowing that David Rudderman knew. Connelly, however, liked his second act and kept it unchanged, and thus the preparation for it was still needed.

Such changes as were made, seemingly, were an attempt to remove the 1938 date from the play; but, in fact, they simply caused confusion. Connelly was apparently aware of the problem, and the second major change was made in the conclusion. In *The Land of the Living*, David is forced to learn that he can not live in Serenity; and he accepts the knowledge without gladness, but with a resolve to do what he can with a bad situation. In *There Are Two Points*, the entire adventure in Serenity proves to be a dream; and David bounces back into the present, no more affected by this dream than by any normal nightmare.

It would seem, as *The Flowers of Virtue* and *A Story for Strangers* suggest, that between 1938 and the mid-1940's, Connelly had second thoughts about the nature of the machine age. True, America had not become a safer place to live; but it was a more joyful place, a more comfortable place; and Connelly has always been more concerned with happiness than with safety. To be sure, he was—and is—still searching for paradise; and Eden had been located in Serenity in the 1938 script. The fault with the play is not in the original script; rather, it lies with Connelly's decision in 1938 to produce *Everywhere I Roam*, rather than *The Land of the Living*. By 1952, when he finished the revisions, or by 1958, when he staged the new version, a different kind of Eden was needed. In the depression, a walled-in land of the past with purpose and employment may have served as a barrier against the corruption of the modern world. By 1952 or 1958, there was no way to wall out the corruption of the modern world, unless the walls were made of lead, seven feet thick.

III The Portable Yenberry[15]

Connelly's most recent play is *The Portable Yenberry,* copyrighted on January 6, 1961, and produced the following year, from May 24 to June 1, at the Purdue University workshop in Lafayette, Indiana. The play was obviously produced for two purposes: first, it gave Purdue University graduate and undergraduate students an opportunity to work in a play under Mr. Connelly's professional direction and, second, to do so with such actors and actresses as Mildred Dunnock—the original Mrs. Hubbard in Lillian Hellman's *Another Part of the Forest*—Burt Brinckerhoff, and Steven Geray. Mr. Connelly also took a role, that of an 1865 physician. Although the program for this showing is labeled "The World Premiere,"[16] Mr. Connelly says that it was merely "an elaborate patchwork rehearsal ... with the majority of the cast amateur." He has, in fact, rewritten the play entirely; and there are serious plans to stage *The Portable Yenberry* in New York sometime in the near future.

Judging from the unfavorable responses given Mr. Connelly's three previous plays—*The Flowers of Virtue, A Story for Strangers,* and *Hunter's Moon*—any producer may, of course, have serious doubts about how well this latest Connelly play would be received. The play is entirely modern in its outlook and wonderfully well constructed; but, as Mr. Connelly is well aware, *The Portable Yenberry* has a hopeful view of man that still, oddly enough, seems old-fashioned in the modern theater of New York.

If, however, university and community theaters ever break with Broadway, ever start doing those plays that represent their views and interests, that make the theater an extension of the rational view of the classroom—"the proper use of the theatre" for society that Connelly has urged for many years—*The Portable Yenberry* will probably be popular. The play, in essence, is concerned with the academic world in academic terms—its notions of science, its notions of history, its notions of theater. It is a play, moreover, that reflects a fondness and respect for that world. As a part of the record of Connelly's literary career, *The*

Portable Yenberry is, also, of some interest for what it shows of his playwriting habits and convictions. In this play, he returns to subjects, characters, and themes from earlier plays.

In an "Author's Note" on the program for the Purdue production of *The Portable Yenberry,* Connelly explains his several purposes in writing the play. "As all kinds of questions are on humanity's lips these days," he wrote in his best Kenneth-Mercer style, "it is possible that some unusually inquisitive soul may want to know what *The Portable Yenberry* is about. Well, friend, I'll tell you." Connelly's explanation suggests a grim seriousness not easily found in the text of the play.

> Indirectly [he wrote] it is a comment on what science and other influences are doing today to scare the pants off contemporary man. Daily—you might even say hourly—alterations of our physical, political, economic, philosophical and spiritual concepts are causing the only world we've known to rocket into an unimaginable tomorrow at a blinding speed. . . .
>
> Specifically, my play reveals the effects of the future of telekinesodics ... on a sensitive young man who has been breeding bait worms on his impoverished Louisiana plantation.
>
> When his adventures began to excite me I became so absorbed in writing them down that I failed to follow some of the tenets of ultra-modern playwriting. I forgot to season the dialogue with graphic Anglo-Saxon monosyllables. I also neglected such fashionable thematic requirements as incestuous families, sexual deviates and junkies.

In truth, *The Portable Yenberry* is not much more concerned with an "unimaginable tomorrow" than it is with junkies. Connelly's note ends with the hope that "you'll find some fun in what I've attempted to do"; and this hope—more than any comment on modern science as a threat to humanity—permeates the play. In fact, the new concepts are not "scaring the pants off" Marc Connelly; instead, they are providing answers to some of his old fears. Nor is *The Portable Yenberry* likely to make anyone else more thoughtful about science and the threats it poses.

A great deal of the fun in this play is private; or, at least, it must seem so to the average young or middle-aged theater-goer and play-reader who knows Connelly solely, or primarily, as the author of *The Green Pastures.* Even the program has its "private jokes": Eddie Senz, New York City, is thanked, for example, for Dr. Bingham's "hairdo." Connelly, whose hairline has been a "running gag" on Broadway for forty years, played the role of Dr. Bingham. The heroine has the same name as Mercer's fiancée, and Mr. Mercer's name is mentioned once. Mrs. Pickering tells of her honeymoon with "Mr. Mercer and Dr. Pickering." She also explains, Mr. Connelly told me, "to her shocked audience that there were two different honeymoons."

The Portable Yenberry reflects Connelly's association with university actors, both as a Yale professor and as a lecturer on hundreds of college campuses. The play, in fact, is in part a spoof of collegiate theories of drama. Scene four in the second act, for example, is concerned with a college production of *Macbeth*. The production is a success when the coed originally cast as Lady Macbeth materializes on stage (having just returned from a time-journey) while her understudy is doing the sleepwalking scene. The director is hailed a genius for directing the scene in which "Suddenly ... both sides of a split personality [are] walking in their sleep," thus revealing the real character of Lady Macbeth. In *The Portable Yenberry,* this stroke of genius was an accident beyond the director's control; but, for several years in the 1950's, a number of university theater groups were producing *Othello* with the major characters played by two actors, dividing the roles into two simpler characters, the "jealous" and the "loving" Othello, for example. This device was viewed by many theatrical people as a "theatrical gimmick" that succeeded only in reducing the complex tragic characters of Shakespeare to melodramatic half-characters—an opinion that Mr. Connelly obviously shared, for he gives the role of one half of Lady Macbeth to Mimi, a Japanese exchange student.

Even without a concern for science or a knowledge of the private jokes, a modern campus audience would probably find *The Portable Yenberry* a pleasant evening in the theater, a shrewd—if sometimes obvious—comment upon the academic world.

Like many of Connelly's earlier plays—most notably *The Land of the Living,* this play is concerned with time travel. It is not, however, the travel itself that is attractive, but what can be accomplished in the present by a manipulation of the past. The action of the play centers around Henry Clay Yenberry's trips back and forth between 1962 and 1865 and the effect "in Commencement Week this year" of these trips upon various students and faculty members at Ogden University.

Yenberry is molded from the same clay that Connelly used for Kenneth Mercer and would use again for Newton Bemis in his novel, *A Souvenir from Qam*. He is a student at Ogden and is attempting to learn enough about insect control to save his plantation, *Reve Perdu* ("Lost Dream"). To be graduated from Ogden, he must take a "precognition" test from Dr. Zuckhauser, an expert in "extra-sensory perception experiments." Henry proves to possess "the greatest extra-sensory perception in scientific history," and he is also attuned to the past. Once, in his youth, he overheard a conversation that had taken place a century earlier. Dr. Zuckhauser's experiments send Henry off on a journey into 1865 and involve him in an intrigue with Dr. Bingham and his lovely daughter, Caroline Lou, a couple of Confederate sympathizers in Civil War Washington.

Henry's disappearance from 1962 causes some consternation. Genevieve, his fiancée, fears that he will miss her performance as Lady Macbeth; and her parents are sympathetic. His return, however, causes a great deal of excitement. Genevieve's father, Professor Holster, a Civil War historian, is interested; for he sees in Henry's time travels a wonderful technique for historical research. The Binghams, it seems, lived next door to John Wilkes Booth when he was plotting the assassination of Lincoln. Dr. Zuckhauser is interested in the scientific possibilities of time travel, both for its own sake and because he hopes it will help him have his grant renewed. Mrs. Holster sees in Henry's century-hopping a wonderful chance for her to invest some money in telegraph stock to be left (in 1962) to her daughter. They all urge Henry to make a second trip, and he finally agrees; for the twenty-five dollars promised him by Dr. Zuckhauser will make it possible for him to remain on campus a weekend longer with Genevieve.

The residents of Washington in 1865 accept Henry's appearances and disappearances with a great deal of *savoir faire*. They believe that he is his own great-grandfather, Thunderbolt Harry Yenberry, a Southern military leader; and Caroline Lou falls in love with him at first sight. Henry is puzzled, for, with each trip through time, he loses his memory. He is also something of a puzzle to the Union officers, who are at first suspicious of him as a spy but are finally convinced that he is merely in· nocently insane.

Henry makes his second trip back to 1865 and returns success- fully; but, during his absence, new problems arise in 1962. In a burst of scientific enthusiasm, Dr. Zuckhauser informs the foundation supporting his projects of this experiment. Mr. Pickering, the head of the foundation, favors cutting off his funds immediately; he is certain that Zuckhauser must be either a fraud or insane. Mrs. Pickering—who spent one honey- moon with a man named Mercer—arrives to conduct her own investigation, and offers Henry ten thousand dollars if he will make a third trip, so she may observe it. Genevieve is opposed to another trip; but Henry sees in the offer not merely sal- vation for *Reve Perdu* but a means of freeing Genevieve from a Hollywood career on which she is about to embark. She had planned to become a "Hollywood Star" to raise the money to save the old plantation. When Henry departs for 1865, Gene- vieve hangs on to his arm and goes with him. After a brief adventure in Civil War Washington, he returns to 1962; but Genevieve lingers in 1865. He is about to make a fourth trip to save her when word is received that she has made her return on stage in the middle of *Macbeth*.

And all's well that ends well. Henry and Genevieve save the old plantation and will marry. Caroline Lou, according to the best historical information, did finally wed her Captain Yenberry—the original Thunderbolt Harry. Dr. Zuckhauser gets his foundation grant, and Professor Holster's next book on the Civil War seems likely to be more popular than the last one, for which he has just received his semiannual royalty check of twelve dollars and eighty-five cents.

It is difficult to evaluate *The Portable Yenberry* in the same context with *The Green Pastures* or even with *Merton of the Movies*. As Connelly indicated in his program note, the play is not concerned with the savage, dark side of man; nor is it concerned with any satiric comment about society. In *The Portable Yenberry* Connelly deals with ideas with which man lives and laughs, not with passions that once threatened to destroy him individually and now threaten to destroy the whole species. It is, of course, a play of hope; men will prevail, and lovers will eventually restore their "Lost Dream."

IV   The Riddle[17]

One other play manuscript for this period is of some interest. Sometime in the mid-1950's, probably 1954, Connelly submitted the script of *The Riddle,* "a motion picture play," to the Library of Congress for copyright protection. This copyright manuscript is apparently the only extant copy of the play; and in 1966, when he was queried about the manuscript, Mr. Connelly had no recollection of it. In one respect, *The Riddle,* as a motion-picture script, lies outside the scope of the present study. Such a statement is not made to infer that Connelly's screen writing is not worth serious concern, but simply to acknowledge that Connelly's entire career as a screen writer is beyond my competence and, it is assumed, beyond the interest of the reader concerned with written literature.

Even as a reading script, however, *The Riddle* is an interesting piece of drama. The basic story deals with Tommy Garcia, a New York Puerto Rican, who—during the course of the play—dies a hero in Korea while using the name of his employer, Kempler. The audience does not discover that the dead hero "Kempler" is Tommy Garcia until the end of the motion picture, when the "riddle" is solved. *The Riddle* is a melodramatic mystery, a who-done-it in the tradition of Alfred Hitchcock, with the mystery unfolding from one scene to the next from the point of view of the investigator.

Even in such a conventional piece of pure theatrics, however, Connelly's serious commitment as an artist shines through. In one respect, *The Riddle* is a straight piece of protest drama, asking that Americans take seriously their responsibilities for making the country safe for all its citizens, especially the victimized minorities, like the Puerto Ricans. In another respect, *The Riddle* is another of Connelly's examinations of the nature of the good simple life and another comment on the relationship of native drama to the life of a community.

Puerto Rico is to *The Riddle* what Millersville was to Connelly's earlier play—a place in which the old values are still recognized. Like Millersville, the land has also been corrupted; but the corruption has come, not from quick prosperity, but from a long depression that has forced the natives to move to New York and into a world of violence. The melodramatic form of the play does not permit much serious discussion of the social problems; but Connelly does suggest that the solution lies in a reformation of the Puerto Rican economy rather than in the transportation of Puerto Ricans to an alien society.

Of some interest to those concerned with Connelly's concept of the nature of drama is one scene in *The Riddle.* In a chase sequence, the heroine seeks and finds her lover with a group of University of Puerto Rico actors called *Rondante Theatre.* They are touring Puerto Rico, taking native drama, *Pere Patelin,* to the people. Their performance is so real that the people watch it in the midst of a rainstorm—the plays are given in the open air—oblivious of the rain in the magic of theater. Good drama for Connelly does not assault; instead, it lifts its audience beyond private life.

V First Novel: Eden Reconsidered

When *A Souvenir from Qam*[18] appeared in 1965, Connelly's audience was prepared to be pleased. As Robert Benchley had pointed out after the first showing of *The Green Pastures,* Connelly had a reputation for writing "perfect" works, and anything less was disappointing to him and his audience.[19] Although, in the main, the book got favorable reviews, there was a general feeling of mild disappointment.[20] *A Souvenir from Qam* did not do in fiction what *The Green Pastures* had done in drama.

"It would be pleasant to report a triumph," Maurice Dolbier wrote in the most unfavorable review the book received, "because the American novel can use . . . the warmth and good-natured humor that Mr. Connelly is noted for. . . ." Reviewing the novel in dramatic terms, Dolbier concluded that, in spite of "a promising first act," there is "second and third act trouble." The fault, he "suspects," is that "Mr. Connelly . . . has taken it easier as a novelist than he would ever have dreamed of doing as a dramatist."[21]

Whatever faults *A Souvenir from Qam* has as a novel, it is not that Mr. Connelly "took it easy." In one way or another, the novel had been in progress for almost twenty years. In fact, the failure of the novel to attract favorable attention may stem from Connelly's long concern with it. It is far more intricate and far more carefully wrought than readers of the book jacket are led to expect. This novel is better on second reading than on first. It is a "perfect," if minor, work.

As Dolbier justly commented, the novel does have a framework that suggests "those admirable Hollywood romantic comedies of the Thirties"; but, within this framework, Connelly again deals with a problem that has concerned him for more than forty years—the road to Eden. Like the romantic comedies of Hollywood or the Restoration English comedies of manners, *A Souvenir from Qam* moves quickly from short scene to short scene, tracing the adventures of Connelly's protagonist, Newton Bemis, as he discovers something about himself and his place in time. Newton is probably related to the Bemises of *The Wisdom Tooth* and *The Flowers of Virtue;* but, unlike them, he lives in the future, rather than in the past, although, to be sure, some of his concepts of virtue seem to belong to the mythical age of American innocence.

Like James Leland of *Little Old Millersville,* Newton is anxious to return to a part of the past, which for him is an old-fashioned home in Vermont, "a dwelling place in which a family could grow," but a home which is also a symbol of accomplishment. It was the home his father had wanted, but which he was unable to buy because he lost his savings through the dishonesty of his partner. Although Newton has a "concentration quotient . . . exactly that of Dr. Robert Oppenheimer," he is still an innocent in the sophisticated way of the world. Until he is seduced by Rowena McGravey, he is a virgin. He is a man afraid of debts. He is scrupulously honest, refusing a million-dollar fee; for he knows his services are not worth it.

Newton's problem is to find the proper mate, one in whom the charm of the past may be combined with the idealism of the future. His first romantic involvement in the novel is with Rowena, the daughter of the millionaire Senator McGravey— a "humour" name from Connelly's Algonquin years. Rowena is beautiful, experienced, intelligent. She fixes upon Newton as a young man of promise; and, after she seduces him, she sets about to remake him in terms of the standards of a materialistic society. Newton is obviously on his way to corruption, for the brief—and cold-blooded—seduction demonstrates that he is no match for her. His friend, Timmy Thackery, describes him as a man who is "essentially an idealist convinced that despite today's grim realities, the indomitable virtue in man's nature will eventually halt his career of self-destruction."

In many ways like the hero of *Land of the Living,* Newton hopes to find a place in which the "indomitable virtues" can again flourish. When he brings Rowena to his home in Vermont, however, it is made quite clear that, with her, the old virtues will be given little consideration. She not only rearranges the Vermont house, thus destroying its inherent value; but she plans to move Newton into a million-dollar New York mansion.

Her solution to the problem—getting the money for Newton for the mansion—comes with an offer from the King of Suruk of a million dollars to Newton as a consulting fee. Newton, for a brief time, frustrates her plans when he informs her that he has no intention of going to Qam (pronounced Gum), the capital of Suruk, and that, if he did go, he would not accept the fee. Rowena, who suspects that Newton is simple-minded, works through friends in the State Department to make him believe that he has a patriotic duty to accept the mission. She is convinced that she can later force him to take the money.

In Qam, Newton meets King Sajjid—a figure much like Anna's King of Siam, except that he is entirely well-meaning, kind, and non-sexual. Newton also meets the Princess Farha, European educated, but still an old-fashioned loyal Surukian. Connelly returns to the techniques of *How's the King?* for some of the comic trappings of his characterization of Suruk. In Uric, in that musical comedy, for example, the national anthem is "God Help the King." In Suruk, the national anthem is titled "Allah Destroy Those Scabrous Dog-Sons of Harlots Who Have Dared Challenge the Might of Holy Suruk," and it is described as ". . . a musical battlecry calling for wild, ear-splitting screams and instrumental notes in about equal parts."

Behind the musical-comedy humor, however, Connelly is seriously concerned with the problems of virtue. Qam is an experimental laboratory in which Sajjid hopes to create a virtuous society. By tradition, Qam is said to have been built on the site of the Garden of Eden; and, when Newton first hears this, he remembers a Sunday School lesson from his youth, taught by "Gentle Mr. Wingate. He was dead now. And so was his world [the world of the literal Garden of Eden] of simple faith." The problem for Suruk is one of living by Mr. Wingate's rules of "simple faith." King Sajjid is entirely benevolent, but simple goodness is not enough. Sajjid himself recognizes this fact when an improperly built schoolhouse collapses and kills thirty children, including his own favorite son.

Sajjid realizes that the problem for ancient Eden in the modern world is to learn the wisdom of the new world without losing the values of the old. He plans to educate himself to this task by travelling about the United States incognito, as a "soda jerk." But Newton does not recognize his problem so clearly. He knows the modern world—in fact, as a scientist, he even knows the facts of the world of tomorrow—but he can find no way to live by the virtues of the past. He is not a native of the Garden of Eden.

Both Sajjid and Newton make progress. Sajjid uncovers a plot to destroy his kingdom, discovers a few of the good rules of modern society (marriages for love, for example), and is ready to begin his travels in America. After a series of adventures, out of the romantic comedies of the 1930's, Newton eventually weds Farha. (Rowena, convinced that Newton is a "half-witted cub scout," breaks their engagement.) The marriage will be a good one, as Farha's aunt, the Princess Budur, tells Newton: "You, my dear boy, have a great deal of your being in the future. And part of Farha is still lingering in the long-ago. I think you both will have a happy adventure sharing today."

In *A Souvenir from Qam,* more than in any other work, Connelly has solved the problem of Eden. Forty years earlier, in *Little Old Millersville,* he demonstrated that he knew the futility of attempting to return to the past; and, in spite of the fact that in *The Wisdom Tooth, Everywhere I Roam,* and *Land of the Living* he kept trying, he was brought back to the here-and-now with a bump. In all of his works that move back in time, Connelly dealt honestly with the problem, acknowledging that, quite aside from the brute necessity of living in the present, life today has much to offer. The present, however, compared nostalgically with the past, had always seemed to lack idealism—the sense of purpose, the courage, of that simpler long-ago.

Material prosperity and the present have never been quite the villains in Connelly's plays that the *Time* reviewer of *Everywhere I Roam* complained that Connelly made them. If, in such a play as *Land of the Living*, Connelly left a statement about the present for the curtain line, it was not because he rejected modern life. Rather, it was that he thought the present could be enriched by a reminder of the virtues of the past that modern life had neglected. It is not material wealth, for example, that Connelly opposes, but materialism. Materialism corrupts Eden; and virtue, even with poverty, is better than corruption. Best of all, as he tried to demonstrate in *A Story for Strangers,* is material plenty *and* virtue.

In *A Souvenir from Qam,* however, Connelly has conjured up a protagonist who is a modern man "with one foot in tomorrow," but one who, at the same time, retains a respect for the past. Bemis' heroes (and Connelly's, too) in this novel are not the pioneers of the past, nor the supermen of tomorrow; they are, rather, men of the day like Dr. Oppenheimer and Adlai Stevenson. Connelly uses Stevenson's name just once in the novel, and its purpose is to demonstrate that wisdom and integrity are still possible in the modern world.[22] Today's Eden, in *A Souvenir from Qam,* has become a hope for the future, based on a conviction that man's good will and honesty are demonstrated by men like Adlai Stevenson and Newton Bemis. The present, with such men, is taking care of itself.

A Souvenir from Qam does contain the "warmth and good-natured humor" that Mr. Dolbier asks for in the modern novel. The comedy-of-manners form that Connelly has used—with its echoes of Algonquin wit—has a tendency, however, to obscure the humanistic purpose if one equates "warmth" with homespun characters. The jokes, it must be admitted, perhaps are too many and too conventional—a complaint also leveled against Congreve's *The Way of the World* following its first performance—but they are not meaningless. In one scene, for example, Connelly shows a "local theatrical," the ladies of the court in a burlesque. To dramatize poorly—as the characters did in *Little Old Millersville*—is to be pretentious, to lose understanding with shoddy imitation; but to burlesque well—as the ladies do in *A Souvenir from Qam*—is to liberate the mind. It is finally this liberty—this freedom from an internal subservience to externals, not a mere rearrangement of externals—that marks a person for citizenship in Eden. Rowena, with her sexual freedom, is yet "addicted to externalities"; Farha, although legally a piece of property, is intellectually free. To live decently, to live honestly, is to live well; and such a life is less a matter of time and place than it is of a sense of idealistic purpose.

The finely spun texture of the novel—with its Algonquin humor, its 1930 romantic-comedy intrigues, its sentimental-comedy characterization—makes the reader, at first, expect less of the novel; but rereading and reconsideration make it apparent that in form, as well as in theme, Connelly is consciously using the familiar and the comfortable to prove his point. The old externals are still there—as they are in Farha's outward habits—but they are the ·means to a new consideration of the future.

VI *Some Tentative Conclusions*

Any conclusions about Marc Connelly's contributions to American literature, of course, must be tentative. Styles in American literature, and especially in the drama, have changed radically in the past twenty years; and, if we assume these changes are permanent, Eugene O'Neill seems likely to be the only American playwright before World War II who will receive major critical attention in the future.

The Green Pastures, to be sure, even by current standards of criticism, holds a position as one of the important plays in American drama; but it is the only one of Connelly's plays that does. A few others—*Beggar on Horseback, The Wisdom Tooth,* and *The Farmer Takes a Wife*—are still given some attention as competent examples of minor forms—"Expressionistic" fantasy and sentimental comedy. Several others—*Dulcy, To the Ladies!, Merton of the Movies,* and *The Traveler*—are interesting both as artifacts of an age and as "other works" by the author of *The Green Pastures.* For Connelly's fiction, even including *A Souvenir from Qam,* the same claims may be made; they are "other works" and may be viewed as artifacts of an age.

In considering current styles of criticism and Connelly's works, however, we should be aware that critical dicta are even more perishable than "minor" literary works. We have merely to reflect upon the history of the critical responses to such works as Etherege's *Man of Mode,* Pope's *Rape of the Lock,* and Congreve's *The Way of the World* to be justly suspicious.

Anyone "making a case" for Connelly's works as literature could, of course, point to his collaborations with Kaufman and argue that these plays did—as Quinn commented—introduce into the American theater a new kind of comedy, a form that still survives with a considerable amount of public approval in such plays as Herb Gardner's *A Thousand Clowns,* Neil Simon's *Odd Couple,* and Gore Vidal's *Visit to a Small Planet,* for examples. We could also argue that in such plays as *Beggar on Horseback* and *The Wisdom Tooth* Connelly popularized theatrical devices that have helped to liberate the stage from the tight confines of the picture frame. *The Green Pastures,* as all the critics noted in 1930, demonstrated that the "art" play could also be commercially successful. Such arguments, however, are aside from the point. Connelly is not a revolutionist in the drama, nor is he the founder of a "new school" of dramatic writing. It is doubtful if even a single "important" playwright in the last twenty years has turned to any of Connelly's plays for models.

At the same time, however, if Connelly has few imitators, he has many "students." There are dozens of writers who have acknowledged their debt to him, both for the direction he gave their work when they studied under him at Yale and for the encouragement he gave as a fellow-dramatist on the New York scene. But even if Mr. Connelly were not known except through his plays, we could still see his influence at work. In fact, I asked him, after having discovered the Kenneth Mercer character, if James Thurber borrowed anything from that character for his Walter Mitty. Although Mr. Connelly had little patience with my suggestion—"Mr. Thurber didn't have to borrow anything from anyone." —the least that can be said is that Thurber and Connelly shared a common view of the inner strength of the "born loser."

When a writer "shows how," rather than "tells how," it is

difficult to estimate exactly how much effect he has had. The character of Professor Charles Osman in Howard Lindsay and Russel Crouse's *Tall Story* was so obviously built on a Connelly-conceived character that the playwrights had Mr. Connelly play the role in both the stage and screen versions of the play. The play, however, is not necessarily "a product" of the "Connelly method."

There is little need for any lengthy discussion of Connelly's influence. He has never had the kind of critical or academic reputation that attracts the novice or the imitator. What he has done in his fifty years as a playwright, fiction writer, and essayist is to give moments of pleasure—and perhaps insight—to a great many people. If he has not expounded a profound philosophy of life, if he has not served as a natural legislator for all mankind, he has made many a young girl smile and an old man dream. He has suggested, pleasantly, how people may be decent, kind, honest and well-mannered (albeit without heroic greatness)—even in trying circumstances. He has taught respect for the craft of the writer; and he has been a constant reminder that drama and fiction, whatever else they may be, are also social graces.

In a lecture to the Adelphi College Summer Theatre students a few years ago, Connelly gave his *ars poetica* for the drama. The theater, he argued, has a responsibility to involve people in its ritual. "This is what the Greek theater was all about," he said. "For hours you sat there and were asked unanswerable questions, and like the chorus onstage, you worked the questions over in your mind." Connelly, however, does not mean, he said, that theater involves people because the playwright preaches "from the pulpit, or the editorial page or the politicians' soapbox." Even successful "message" playwrights like T. S. Eliot, Bertolt Brecht, and G. B. Shaw, he argued, do not succeed because of their "lecturing"—their "over-intellectualized patronization" (Eliot); their "abstract argumentation" (Shaw); or their "exhortations" (Brecht)—but in spite of it.

"When the playwright starts saying 'I think,' " Connelly said, "the audience gets up to leave. Does the actor laugh at the joke he makes? No, we do, and the same with the playwright. He can't capture us by telling us what our morals should be.

He can only capture us by giving us the tools with which to examine morals."

"The happiest of all benign drugs," he told the Adelphi College students, "is the theater—good theater."[23] It is the function of this "good theater"—he wrote several years ago—to "shed light, a light governments should keep burning so that at every pause of his journey man may look at himself and by what he sees be encouraged to continue to his destiny."[24]

VII *The Active Mr. Connelly*

During 1966, I spent several weeks talking with Mr. Connelly. He was seventy-five years old, but it was quite obvious to me that anyone writing a book about his literary life would have to leave the last chapter—or two—unwritten. Except for his sense of ease, Mr. Connelly works and thinks like a young man just starting his career. His works-in-progress in the winter of 1967-68 included a new novel that he hoped to have ready for his publisher soon, several essays, his memoirs, and a musical comedy, *Kitty in the City*.

It is, of course, easy to respect the man for his activity and yet expect little of lasting worth to result from it. American literature—and especially drama—has always seemed to be the product of the comparatively young. Anyone who has reviewed Mr. Connelly's career, however, would be bold to make such an assumption. Among the Broadway-wise in the late 1920's, for example, the general opinion was that he had passed his peak—an opinion that must have caused some discomfort with the success of *The Green Pastures*.

Mr. Connelly has three literary contributions: *The Green Pastures;* the "other works" he has done; and the work he is now doing. Only the first of these, at the moment, has much reputation. The prospects for the second seem brighter all the time. As Max Gordon pointed out recently about Connelly's first collaborator, George Kaufman, his ". . . star appeared to be in an eclipse . . . ; [but] today his impact on the theater seems greater than ever."[25] The New York audiences rediscovering Kaufman, it would seem, must soon discover not only the Connelly with Kaufman of such plays as *Merton of the Movies,* but also the pure Connelly of *The Wisdom Tooth.* Then, too, academic critics—and general readers—will eventually find a way to make the unpublished works like *A Story for Strangers* available.

America is developing a group of adult readers—not young readers seeking to find a substitute for experience, but older readers now concerned with reconsiderations to make. As Sophocles in his old age found an audience for his *Oedipus at Colonus,* it is not improbable that American readers and theatergoers will find in Connelly's works of the last twenty years— and in any of his future works—a new cause for being concerned with his art. In both his literary work and in his private life, Mr. Connelly has given thoughtful consideration to what makes the "good life." Few people aware of him would not concede that in his private life, he has discovered many of the secrets. For the thoughtful reader, these secrets are revealed in his literature.

Notes and References

Chapter One

1. The most complete biographical account of Marc Connelly is John Parker, *Who's Who in the Theatre* (New York, 1952), p. 477.

2. Marc Connelly, "A Curtain Rises," *New Yorker*, XXX (December 18, 1954), 120–27.

3. *Ibid.*, 122.

4. *Ibid.*, 122.

5. *Ibid.*, 122.

6. Fred K. Schuller, "How's Everything Back Home? Connelly Hopes To Visit Here," McKeesport, Pennsylvania, *Daily News*, undated clipping (for 1938), in files of McKeesport Public Library.

7. "Famed Playwright Marc Connelly Recalls Childhood in McKeesport," McKeesport *Daily News*, July 5, 1964, 1.

8. Bob Thomas, "Connelly Confesses: I Was Inner-Directed Under-Study," New York *World-Telegram and Sun Feature Magazine*, August 29, 1959, 4.

9. "A Curtain Rises," 120.

10. Harry Altschuler, "A Novel Thing Just Happened," *World-Telegram and Sun Feature Magazine*, June 12, 1965, 17.

11. "Famed Playwright . . . ," 1.

12. *Ibid.*, 8.

13. *Ibid.*, 8.

14. *Ibid.*, 8. Mr. Connelly corrected this piece of information. It was not until he became a reporter for *The Gazette Times* that he made twenty-eight dollars a week, and six of that was for his column, *Jots and Tittles*.

15. Walter Prichard Eaton, "A Playboy Makes Good," New York *Herald Tribune*, March 23, 1930, Magazine Section, 10.

16. "Wartime Children of Germany Turn Reporters of Events," Pittsburgh *Gazette Times*, March 21, 1915, second section, 8.

17. "Farmers Told How to Grow Corn-Cabbage," Pittsburgh *Gazette Times*, January 3, 1915, third section, 5.

18. "The Average American," in *Jots and Tittles*, Pittsburgh *Gazette Times*, September 27, 1914, sixth section, 1.

19. Altschuler, "A Novel Thing Just Happened," 17.

20. Arthur Hobson Quinn, *History of the American Drama from the Civil War to the Present Day* (New York, 1927), II, p. 298.

21. Eaton, "A Playboy Makes Good," 10.

22. *Ibid.*, 10.

23. Tex McCrary and Jinx Falkenburg, "New York Close-up," New York *Herald Tribune*, April 9, 1951, 24.

24. Eaton, "A Playboy Makes Good," 10.

25. Bernard K. Schilling, *The Comic Spirit* (Detroit, 1965), p. 17.

26. "Famous Native Son Captivates Audience with Views of Life, Theater, Early Days," McKeesport *Daily News*, January 27, 1965, 1.

27. The only known, extant copy of *The Lady of Luzon* is the copyright manuscript in the Library of Congress, dated "June 2nd, 1913." The title page is printed: " 'The Lady of Luzon' A Musical comedy in Two Acts—Book by Alfred Ward Birdsall. Music by Zoel Joseph Parenteau. Lyrics by Marc Connelly," and the sixty-two pages of the text are typed. There is, apparently, no longer any copy of *The Amber Princess*, although it was copyrighted.

Chapter Two

1. *The Deep Tangled Wildwood* is extant only in the copyright manuscript in the Library of Congress. The play was copyrighted under the title *Little Old Millersville*, but alternate titles are written on the title page. The book for *Helen of Troy, N. Y.*, for which Bert Kalmar and Harry Ruby wrote the music and lyrics, exists only in the copyright manuscript in the Library of Congress. There is, seemingly, no extant copy of *Be Yourself*. Mr. Connelly told me that he did not have a personal copy.

2. Joseph Mersand, ed., *Three Plays About Business In America* (New York, 1964), p. 87.

3. Quinn, *History of the American Drama*, II, pp. 205–25, evaluates the relative contributions of each man. See, also, Fred B. Millet, *Contemporary American Authors* (New York, 1940), pp. 113–14.

4. Moss Hart, *Act One: An Autobiography* (New York, 1959), p. 350.

5. Margaret Case Harriman, *The Vicious Circle: The Story of the Algonquin Round Table* (New York, 1951), p. 11. The general account of the Algonquin group is taken from this source.

6. Burns Mantle, ed., *Best Plays of 1921–22* (New York, 1922).

7. *Ibid.*, p. v.

8. The most readily available edition of *Dulcy* is French's *Standard Library Edition* (New York, 1950), and all citations from the play are from this edition.

9. Quinn, *History of the American Drama*, II, p. 220.

10. Joseph Wood Krutch, *American Drama Since 1918* (New York, 1957), p. 27.

11. *Ibid.*, p. 136.

12. Edmond M. Gagey, *Revolution in American Drama* (New York, 1947), p. 217.

13. John Gassner, ed., *Twenty-Five Best Plays of the Modern American Theatre* (New York, 1949), p. 124.

14. *To the Ladies!* was first published in Arthur Hobson Quinn, ed., *Contemporary American Plays* (New York, 1923); and since the *French Standard Library Edition* has long been out of print, Quinn's edition is now the most easily available. All citations from the play are from this edition.

15. Harriman, *Vicious Circle*, p. 43.

16. Mantle, ed., *Best Plays of 1921–22*, p. iv.

17. Quinn, *History of the American Drama*, II, p. 220.

18. Quinn, ed., *Contemporary American Plays*, p. xxiv.

19. Cited in Harriman, *Vicious Circle*, p. 99. Mrs. Harriman gives detailed accounts of both *No Sirree!* and *The Forty-Niners.*

20. *Ibid.*, p. 99.

21. Franklin P. Adams, *The Diary of Our Own Samuel Pepys* (New York, 1935), I, p. 335.

22. All cited in Joseph Lawren, ed., *The Drama Year Book 1924* (New York, 1924), p. 87.

23. Adams, *Diary of Our Own Samuel Pepys*, I, p. 433.

24. Lawren, ed., *Drama Year Book 1924*, p. 87.

25. Adams, *Diary of Our Own Samuel Pepys*, I, p. 307.

26. Gassner, ed., *Twenty-Five Best Plays*, p. xxiv.

27. Gagey, *Revolution in American Drama*, p. 217.

28. Krutch, *American Drama Since 1918*, p. 137.

29. Bernard Sobel, "Musical Comedy, Quo Vadis?," *Theatre Arts*, XII (August, 1928), 566–75, credited the "great popularity" of *Helen of Troy, N. Y.* to the fact that it "had a refreshing book that spoofed at musical comedy conventions."

30. Gilbert Seldes, *The Seven Lively Arts* (New York, 1924), p. 13.

31. Cited in Harriman, *Vicious Circle*, p. 105.

32. Quinn, *History of the American Drama*, II, p. 222.

33. Kenneth Macgowan, "From the Four Corners of American Art," *Theatre Arts*, VIII (April, 1924), 220-21.

34. The most easily available edition of *Beggar on Horseback* is in *Three Plays About Business In America*, ed. Joseph Mersand; however, since this edition does not have the special newspaper distributed to the audience as part of the production, the first edition, *Beggar on Horseback: A Play in Two Parts* (New York, 1924), is used for all citations. This first edition contains the introduction by Woollcott. P. 13.

35. *Ibid.*, p. 15.

36. John Gassner, *Form and Idea in Modern Theatre* (New York, 1946), p. 249.

37. Gassner, ed., *Twenty-Five Best Plays*, p. 124.

38. Adams, *Diary of Our Own Samuel Pepys*, I, p. 456.

39. "Dewdrop Man," *Newsweek*, LXV (June 18, 1965), 88. Connelly complained, however, that at times the new playwrights put "an awful lot of reliance on cleverness rather than on real editorial content."

40. Mersand, ed., *Three Plays About Business In America*, p. 88.

41. Quinn, *History of the American Drama*, II, p. 224.

42. Burns Mantle, ed., *Best Plays of 1924–25* (New York, 1925), p. 447, summarizes the play: "Matt McLean (Jack Donahue) sings and dances his way out of a Tennessee feud."

43. The copyright manuscript of *Service*, used for this study, dated 1932, is apparently the only extant copy of the play. Mr. Connelly has no recollection of the work.

Chapter Three

1. See "The Passing of the Thanatopsis," in *Enchanted Aisles* (New York, 1924), for Alexander Woollcott's picture of Connelly as "an innocent."

2. Alexander Woollcott, "Quite a Proposition," *Ladies Home Journal,* LII (September. 1935), 9.

3. Robert Benchley, "What Is a Good Show?," *New Yorker,* VI (March 8, 1930), 28.

4. Eaton, "A Playboy Makes Good," 10.

5. The most readily available edition of *The Wisdom Tooth* is *French's Standard Library Edition* (New York, 1927). All citations from the play are from this edition.

6. Quinn, *History of the American Drama,* II, p. 224.

7. Adams, *Diary of Our Own Samuel Pepys,* II, p. 359.

8. Stark Young, "Wisdom Tooth," *New Republic,* XLVI (March 3, 1926), 45.

9. Millet, *Contemporary American Authors,* p. 114.

10. Lewis twice tried to interest Connelly in collaborating with him on plays. Mark Schorer, *Sinclair Lewis: An American Life* (New York, 1961), p. 369, and *passim.*

11. *The Wild Man of Borneo,* copyrighted August 8, 1927, is now extant only in the copyright manuscript. All citations from the play are from this copy.

12. Burns Mantle, ed., *Best Plays of 1927–28* (New York, 1928), p. 404.

13. John Mason Brown, "The Dull Devil of Melodrama: Broadway in Review," *Theatre Arts,* XI (November, 1927), 821.

14. Stark Young, "Wild Men," *New Republic,* LII (September 28, 1927), 149.

15. Mantle, ed., *Best Plays of 1927–28,* p. 404.

16. See Connelly, "A Curtain Rises," 120–27.

17. John Mason Brown, "Files on Parade; The Season in Prospect," *Theatre Arts,* XI (October, 1927), 744.

18. *How's the King?,* copyrighted 1925, is now extant only in the copyright manuscript. All citations from the play are from this copy. Mr. Connelly has a fragmentary copy in his personal files.

19. The most easily available edition of *The Traveler* is in Bennett Cerf and Van H. Cartmell, eds., *24 Favorite One-Act Plays* (New York, 1958). All citations from the play are from this edition.

20. The copyright manuscript, used for this study, is dated January 26, 1929. It is the only known extant copy of the play.

21. The copyright manuscript, used for this study, is dated 1929. It is the only known extant copy of the play.

22. The copyright manuscript, used for this study, is dated July 29, 1929. It is the only known extant copy of the play.

23. The copyright manuscript, used for this study, is dated July 13, 1929. It is the only known extant copy of the play.

24. John Mason Brown, "Catalogue of Ships," *Theatre Arts,* X (October, 1926), 661.

25. *Ex Cathedra* was twice copyrighted by Connelly, first in 1926 in the form in which it appeared in *Theatre Arts,* X (December, 1926), and again on January 21, 1952, under the title, *Rehearsal for a Feast.* Except for fuller stage directions in the 1952 version and a few minor changes in diction, the play was not changed. All citations to the play are from the *Theatre Arts* version.

26. Harriman, *Vicious Circle*, p. 169.

27. Dale Kramer, *Ross and the New Yorker* (New York, 1951), p. 71.

28. See "Bibliography" for a list of Connelly's nondramatic works in this period.

Chapter Four

1. Adams, *Diary of Our Own Samuel Pepys*, II, p. 854.

2. "On the Fringe: Answers from the Authors," *Saturday Review*, XLVIII (July 24, 1965), 40.

3. *Ibid.*, 40. Connelly's own account in this article and another description (Schuller, "How's Everything Back Home? Connelly Hopes To Visit Here") refute Alexander Woollcott's account in "Quite a Proposition," in which he argued that Connelly's knowledge of the Louisiana scene was "only such as he might have acquired during two weeks spent foraging for local color in New Orleans . . . ." 9.

4. "On the Fringe," 40.

5. See Edith J. R. Isaacs, *The Negro in American Theatre* (New York, 1947), for an account of the part *The Green Pastures* played in the acceptance of the Negro actor in the commercial theater.

6. Burns Mantle, ed., *Best Plays of 1929–30* (New York, 1930), p. viii.

7. Five years later, when *The Green Pastures* returned to New York after an unbroken run, *Variety* published its original prophecy again. "They were good sports about it," Mr. Connelly commented.

8. Francis Fergusson, " 'The Green Pastures' Revisited," *Bookman*, LXXIII (May, 1931), 194.

9. Burns Mantle, ed., *Best Plays of 1942–43* (New York, 1943), p. 29.

10. "The Pulitzer Blues," *Literary Digest*, CV (May 31, 1930), 19–20.

11. *The New York Times Index* for the years from 1930 to 1934 lists over twenty-five different major news stories concerning the play, including accounts of long runs, biographical sketches, and various attempts at censorship in both the United States and Europe.

12. John Chapman, ed., *Best Plays of 1950–51* (New York, 1951), p. 11.

13. John Mason Brown, *Dramatis Personae* (New York, 1963), p. 88.

14. *Ibid.*, pp. 88–89.

15. *The Green Pastures*, Vincent Long, ed., (London, 1963).

16. Joseph Wershba, "Daily Closeup: Marc Connelly," New York *Post*, March 5, 1959, 54.

17. John Gassner, ed., *A Treasury of the Theatre* (New York, 1960), p. 896.

18. E. Bradlee Watson and Benfield Pressey, eds., *Contemporary Drama: Eleven Plays* (New York, 1956), p. 45.

19. Ward Morehouse, "Broadway After Dark: Prof Connelly (Yale) Talks of 'Pastures'," New York *Sun*, February 1, 1951, 20.

20. The first edition of *The Green Pastures* (New York, 1929) went through over a dozen printings and is still generally available. All citations from the play are from this edition.

21. *The Green Pastures*, Long, ed., p. ix.

22. Mr. Connelly commented on this interpretation: "Reason for little boy's inquiry is news to me. My feeling was the little boy was just interested in how old Adam was."

23. Paul T. Nolan, "God on Stage: A Problem in Characterization; Marc Connelly's *Green Pastures,*" *Xavier University Studies,* IV (May, 1965), 75–84.

24. Vincent Long, in his edition of the play, argues that "If we disapprove of this anthropomorphism [in *The Green Pastures*] we must also repudiate our own religious origins, including much of the Bible." P. ix.

Chapter Five

1. Heywood Broun, "*The Green Pastures,*" New York *Telegraph,* February 28, 1930: reprinted in George Oppenheimer, *Passionate Playgoer* (New York, 1958), pp. 547-49.

2. Robert Wilkington, "Note on the Corpus Christi Plays and 'The Green Pastures'," *Shakespeare Association Bulletin,* IX (1934), 173–97. This was the first time that scholars had given any of Mr. Connelly's work serious attention.

3. "We're Going To Have Better Plays," *Theatre Magazine,* LII (December 30, 1930), 16, 63–64.

4. New York *Times,* March 15, 1933, 20.

5. Ward Morehouse, "Broadway After Dark," New York *Sun,* February 1, 1944, 20. See *Best Plays* editions for years from 1930 through 1935 for records of production.

6. Burns Mantle, ed., *Best Plays of 1934-35* (New York, 1935), p. 262.

7. E. Baird Shurman, *Robert E. Sherwood* (New York, 1960), p. 8.

8. Caspar H. Nannes, *Politics in American Drama* (Washington, D. C., 1960), p. 232.

9. Woollcott, "Quite a Proposition," 9.

10. Woollcott was surprised when Connelly told him that he considered the description the "meanest, cruelest, and most malicious thing" that had ever been written about him; however, according to Beatrice Kaufman and Joseph Hennessey, Connelly did not hold "the grudge" long, for he later commented that Woollcott, "... like all wholehearted lovers," often did things "which seemed absurd to less stimulated people." *Letters of Alexander Woollcott* (New York, 1944), p. 171.

11. Altschuler, "A Novel Thing Just Happened," 17.

12. Elliot Nugent, *Events Leading Up To The Comedy* (New York, 1965), p. 145.

13. Naomi Jolles, "A Chemist on the Stage," New York *Post Daily Magazine,* January 24, 1944, 1.

14. Wershba, "Daily Closeup: Marc Connelly," 54. Joseph Wood Krutch, *American Drama Since 1918,* p. 209, credits Connelly's practice with being the model for the "gentle shrewdness" of the play. S. J. Perelman's fanciful essay, "Arthur Kober" (reprinted in George Oppenheimer, *Passionate Playgoer,* pp. 288–94), deals at length with Connelly's "discovery" of *Having Wonderful Time.* Although the account is half-fictional, it does demonstrate the high regard in which Connelly was held for his work with this play.

15. John Mason Brown, "Two on the Aisle: Mr. Connelly and Mr. Blau Stage 'Everywhere I Roam'," New York *Post,* January 8, 1939, 6.

16. Watson and Pressey, eds., *Contemporary Drama: Eleven Plays,* p. 46.

17. Wershba, "Daily Closeup: Marc Connelly," 54.

Notes and References

18. *The Unemployed Ghost,* copyrighted in 1931, was produced by RKO with Connelly playing the lead. It has never been published. The only extant copy is the copyright manuscript used for this study.

19. *The Little Duchess,* copyrighted May 22, 1934, was produced by RKO. It has never been published. The only extant copy is the copyright manuscript used for this study.

20. An abridged edition of *The Farmer Takes a Wife* was published in Mantle, ed., *Best Plays of 1934–35.* The only known extant copy of the entire play is the copyright manuscript, dated September 28, 1934, and used for this study.

21. Mantle, ed., *Best Plays of 1934–35,* p. 262.

22. "The Drama Dons Its Motley for the Season," *Literary Digest,* CXX (September 21, 1935), 20.

23. John Hutchens called *Mr. Gilhooley* "the strongest and most theatrically satisfying" new play of the season. "Books Into Plays: Broadway in Review," *Theatre Arts,* XIV (December, 1930), 1003.

24. Mantle, ed., *Best Plays of 1934–35,* p. 358.

25. *Ibid.,* p. 262.

26. *Ibid.,* p. 263.

27. "New Plays in Manhattan," *Time,* XXXIII (January 9, 1939), 25. *Everywhere I Roam* was given a WPA production in April, 1938; but there was not a commercial production until December, 1938. "WPA Experimental Production," New York *Times,* April 22, 1938, 15.

28. Brown, "Two on the Aisle: Mr. Connelly and Mr. Blau Stage 'Everywhere I Roam'," 6.

29. Burns Mantle, ed., *Best Plays of 1938–39* (New York, 1939), p. 8.

30. Nugent, *Events Leading Up To The Comedy,* p. 145.

31. James Boyd, ed., *The Free Company Presents ... A Collection of Plays About The Meaning Of America* (New York, 1941).

32. *Ibid.,* p. 26.

33. "Notes on How To Produce 'The Free Company' Plays," *ibid.,* pp. 51ff.

34. The only known extant copy of *The Land of the Living* is the copyright manuscript, dated 1938, and used for this study.

35. The only known extant copy of *There Are Two Points* is the copyright manuscript, dated 1952, and used for this study. It is this version of the play that was produced in 1958 under the title *Hunter's Moon.*

36. "Hunter's Moon by M. Connelly: London," New York *Times,* March 16, 1958, 3.

Chapter Six

1. Burns Mantle, ed., *Best Plays of 1937–38* (New York, 1938), p. 466.

2. Mantle, ed., *Best Plays of 1938–39,* p. 448.

3. Connelly during these years spent much of his time "flying back and forth between New York and Hollywood where he is one of the highest paid writers...." "Connelly in Quest for 'New Harrison'," McKeesport *Daily News,* February 4, 1944, 1.

4. "Marc Connelly's 'Flowers of Virtue' Comes To Royale Theatre Thursday," New York *Sun,* February 1, 1942, 20.

5. *Ibid.,* 20.

6. Robert Warnock, ed., *Representative Modern Plays American* (Chicago, 1952), p. 14.

7. Burns Mantle, ed., *Best Plays of 1941–42* (New York, 1942), p. 11.

8. *Ibid.*, p. 438.

9. Rosamond Gilder, "Places and People," *Theatre Arts*, XXVI (April, 1942), 225.

10. George Freedley, "The Stage Today: Marc Connelly's 'Flowers of Virtue' Has Many Bright, Humorous Spots," New York *Morning Telegraph*, February 6, 1942, 22.

11. Frank Farrell, "Theatre: The Flowers of Virtue That Bloom Tra-la-la," New York *Post*, February 6, 1942, 28.

12. Freedley, "The Stage Today: Marc Connelly's 'Flowers of Virtue' ...," 22.

13. Mantle, ed., *Best Plays of 1941–42*, p. 8.

14. In fact, Connelly did not even copyright the play until 1945.

15. The only known extant copy of *The Flowers of Virtue* is the typed copyright manuscript, dated January 10, 1945, used for this study.

16. Farrell, "Theatre: The Flowers of Virtue That Bloom Tra-la-la," 28.

17. "Connelly in Quest for 'New Harrison'," 1.

18. John Chapman, "Marc Connelly, Martha Scott Illumine 'Our Town' at Center," New York *Daily News*, January 1, 1944, 26.

19. Ward Morehouse, "Broadway After Dark: 'Green Pastures'? ... Find the Actor!," New York *Sun*, February 1, 1944, Amusement Section, 20.

20. Marc Connelly, "The Most Unforgettable Character I've Met," *Reader's Digest*, LXXXVI (May, 1965), 78.

Chapter Seven

1. Burns Mantle, ed., *Best Plays of 1944–45* (New York, 1945), p. 415.

2. Chapman, ed., *Best Plays of 1950–51*, p. 11.

3. "Hunter's Moon," *London Observer*, March 2, 1958, 28.

4. "City's Marc Connelly in Defenders Series," McKeesport *Daily News*, November 11, 1963, 4.

5. Allan Lewis, *American Plays and Playwrights of the Contemporary Theatre* (New York, 1965), p. 257.

6. *A Story for Strangers*, except for copies in Mr. Connelly's personal files, exists only in the typed manuscript of the copyright copy, dated 1948, used for this study. All citations from the play are from this copy.

7. "Divine Comedian," *Time*, XLIX (May 19, 1947), 80.

8. "The Theater," *Time*, LII (October 4, 1948), 59.

9. Joseph Wood Krutch, "Drama," *Nation*, CLVII (October 2, 1948), 381.

10. Kappo Phelan, "The Stage & Screen: *A Story for Strangers*," *Commonweal*, XLIII (October 8, 1948), 618.

11. Wolcott Gibbs, "Just Louder, Not Funny," *New Yorker*, XXIV (October 2, 1948), 51.

12. *There Are Two Points* was copyrighted in 1952, and all citations from the play are from the copyright manuscript. The title of the play is taken from Robert Browning's *Paracelsus:* "Are there not, dear Michael/ Two points in the adventure of the diver,/ One—when, a beggar, he prepares to plunge,/ One—when a prince, he rises with his pearl?"

13. An unsigned review in the *London Observer* suggests the reasons that Connelly did not bring the play to New York. The play, the reviewer wrote, "has three full sets by Timothy O'Brien as beautiful as any I have seen in many months. What happens in front of them is swooningly stupid."

14. According to the reviewer, the action deals with "A modern aviator" who "happens (or stumbles or crashes ...) on a New England village which has survived intact for two centuries, speaking bad blank verse. . . . The moral is that we should live in the present, and the general effect is that of a musical *a la* 'Brigadoon' or even 'Plain and Fancy' from which the composer has suddenly, in a fit of justified pique, withdrawn the score."

15. *The Portable Yenberry* was copyrighted January 6, 1961, and all citations from the play are from the copyright manuscript. Mr. Connelly told me that the play has been "completely revised."

16. The four-page program for *The Portable Yenberry* includes the cast, "Author's Notes," a "Who's Who" of the principals, and "Special Credits."

17. The copyright manuscript of *The Riddle,* used for this study, is not dated; but internal evidence suggests 1954 as the most probable date of composition.

18. Marc Connelly, *A Souvenir from Qam* (New York, 1965), 192 pp. All citations from the novel are from this edition.

19. Benchley, "What Is a Good Show?," 27–30. Benchley argued that Connelly's standards were so high that any audience expected more from him than other playwrights. Connelly's plays, he wrote, were superior to Shaw's *Apple Cart,* which was being shown at the time.

20. For the most part, the reviewers merely noted the book, although they did have complimentary comments about various aspects of the novel. See reviews in *Atlantic,* CCXVI (September, 1965), 145; *New Yorker,* XLI (August 14, 1965), 119; and *Saturday Review,* XLVIII (June 26, 1965), 40, for examples. Mr. Connelly told me that he and his publisher were both pleased with the general reception given his first novel.

21. Maurice Dolbier, "A Novel Failure for a Playwright," New York *Herald Tribune,* June 7, 1965, 24. Dolbier's review is the longest discussion given the novel. Many of the general essays that appeared simply used *A Souvenir from Qam* as a news event for a "feature lead" for a biographical account of Connelly's career.

22. Adlai Stevenson, after reading the novel, wrote to Connelly, expressing his pleasure with his "minor role" in *A Souvenir from Qam.* He enjoyed the role, he wrote, more than many "major roles" he had played elsewhere.

23. Michael Janeway, "Marc Connelly High on Happy Drama," *Newsday,* August 1, 1963, 14.

24. Marc Connelly, "The Life of the Theatre," *Saturday Review,* XXXVII (October 23, 1954), 43.

25. "My Most Unforgettable Character," *Reader's Digest,* LXXXX (March, 1967), 180.

Selected Bibliography

Marc Connelly has been a professional writer for over fifty years and is still active. The University of Wisconsin has been named as the official repository for his manuscripts, but at the present time there has been little effort to collect, sort, or identify all of them. Only about one-third of the plays have been published thus far, and a few of his produced plays may no longer be extant in any form. This bibliography includes a few titles of works for which there is no known extant manuscript, such items being marked with an asterisk (*). Although the principal intention in the "Primary Sources" section is to give a complete list of Connelly's "more important works," some of the lesser works—general articles and reviews—have been included to indicate the range of his writing activities.

PRIMARY SOURCES

1. *Plays* (Listed Chronologically)

The Lady of Luzon. Musical comedy in two acts. (Book by A. W. Birdsall. Music by Zoel Joseph Parenteau.) Lyrics by Marc Connelly. Copyright ms., June 2, 1913, 62 typed pp., is only known manuscript.

*The Amber Princess. Operetta in three acts. Book and lyrics by M. Connelly. (Music by Zoel Parenteau.) Copyrighted April 19, 1916. No known copy.

Dulcy. Comedy in three acts by George S. Kaufman and Marc Connelly. New York: G. P. Putnam's Sons, 1921. "Introduction" by Booth Tarkington. New York: Samuel French, 1923. Included in: Helen L. Cohen, ed. *Longer Plays by Modern Authors (American).* New York: Harcourt, Brace & Co., 1922; Montrose J. Moses, ed. *Representative American Dramas: National and Local.* New York: Little, Brown & Co., 1925; and, in abridged form, in Burns Mantle, ed. *Best Plays of 1921–22.* New York: Dodd, Mead and Company, 1922.

To the Ladies! Comedy in three acts by George S. Kaufman and Marc Connelly. Arthur Hobson Quinn, ed. *Contemporary American Plays.* New York: Charles Scribner's Sons, 1923. New York: Samuel French, 1924.

Little Old Millersville. Comedy in prologue and three acts by George S. Kaufman and Marc Connelly. (Variously titled: *Freedom of the City, Turn to the Left, West of Pittsburgh,* and *The Deep Tangled Wildwood.*) Copyright ms., 1921, 138 typed pp., is only known manuscript.

Merton of the Movies. A dramatization of Harry Leon Wilson's story of the same name. By George S. Kaufman and Marc Connelly. New York: Samuel French, 1925. Included, in abridged form, in Burns Mantle, ed. *Best Plays of 1922–23.* New York: Dodd, Mead and Company, 1923.

Beggar on Horseback. A Play in Two Parts. By George S. Kaufman and Marc Connelly. New York: Boni and Liveright, 1924. "Preface" by Alexander Woollcott. Included in: John Gassner, ed. *Twenty-Five Best Plays of the Modern American Theatre.* New York: Crown Publishers, 1949; Robert Warnock, ed. *Representative Modern Plays American.* Chicago: Scott, Foresman and Company, 1952; Joseph Mersand, ed. *Three Plays About Business In America.* New York: Washington Square Press, 1964; and, in abridged form, Burns Mantle, ed. *Best Plays of 1923–24.* New York: Dodd, Mead and Company, 1924.

Helen of Troy, N. Y. Musical comedy in two acts. Book by George S. Kaufman and Marc Connelly. (Music and lyrics by Bert Kalmar and Harry Ruby.) Copyright ms., 1923, 123 typed pp., is only known manuscript.

*Be Yourself. Musical comedy by George S. Kaufman and Marc Connelly. No record of copyright and no known extant copy. Produced in New York, September, 1924.

How's the King? Prologue and three acts. Musical comedy. Copyright ms., 1925, 111 typed pp., is only known manuscript.

Ex Cathedra: A Monographic Pantomime. Theatre Arts Monthly, X (December, 1926), 844–48. Slightly altered version, *Rehearsal for the Feast,* exists in copyright ms., January 21, 1952, 25 typed pp.

The Wisdom Tooth. Fantastic comedy in three acts. New York: Samuel French, 1927; and, in abridged form, Burns Mantle, ed. *Best Plays of 1925–26.* New York: Dodd, Mead and Company, 1926.

The Traveller. (Also spelled *Traveler.*) A one-act sketch. *New Yorker,* II (April 17, 1926), 17–19; New York: Dramatists Play Service, Inc., 1937 (out-of-print); and in Bennett Cerf and Van H. Cartmell, eds. *24 Favorite One-Act Plays.* New York: Doubleday & Company, Inc., 1958.

The Wild Man of Borneo. Comedy by Marc Connelly and Herman J. Mankiewicz. Copyright ms., August 8, 1927, 101 typed pp., is only known manuscript.

The Bridegroom. One-act play. Copyright ms., January 26, 1929, 5 typed pp., is only known manuscript.

The Uncle. One-act play. Copyright ms., July 13, 1929, 7 typed pp., is only known manuscript.

The Suitor. One-act play. Copyright ms., July 29, 1929, 6 typed pp., is only known manuscript.

The Burglar. One-act sketch. Copyright ms., 1929, 8 typed pp., is only known manuscript.

The Green Pastures: A Fable. "Suggested by Roark Bradford's Southern Sketches, 'Ol' Man Adam an' His Chillun'." New York: Farrar & Rinehart, Inc., 1929. This play has been republished in over thirty different editions and anthologies, of which the following are representative: *French's Standard Library Edition,* 1932; Katherine Coe and William H. Cordell, eds. *Pulitzer Prize Plays.* New York: Random House, 1940; E. Bradlee Watson and Benfield Pressey, eds. *Contemporary Drama: Eleven Plays.* New York: Charles Scribner's Sons, 1956; John Gassner, ed. *A Treasury of the Theatre: From Henrik Ibsen to Eugene Ionesco.* New York: Simon and Schuster, 1960; Vincent Long, ed. *The Green Pastures.* "With critical essays by W. R. Matthews, John Macmurray, and Henry

Self." London: Delisle, 1963; and, in abridged form, Burns Mantle, ed. *Best Plays of 1929–30.* New York: Dodd, Mead and Company, 1930. Mr. Connelly's own redaction, "This Play's the Thing: Green Pastures," was published in *Theatre Magazine,* LII (May, 1930), 32–35 and 66–70.

The Unemployed Ghost. One-act play. Copyright ms., 1931, 6 typed pp., is only known manuscript.

Service. By George S. Kaufman and Marc Connelly. Copyright ms., 1932, 9 typed pp., is only known manuscript.

"The Survey." *New Yorker,* VIII (May 12, 1934), 18–19.

The Little Duchess. One-act play. Copyright ms., May 22, 1934, 8 typed pp., is only known manuscript.

The Farmer Takes a Wife. "Based on the novel, 'Rome Haul' by Walter D. Edmonds." By Marc Connelly and Frank D. Elser. Abridgement in Burns Mantle, ed., *Best Plays of 1934–35.* New York: Dodd, Mead and Company, 1935. Copyright ms., September 28, 1934, 92 typed pp., is the only known complete manuscript.

Little David. Scene from *The Green Pastures.* New York: Dramatists Play Service, 1937.

Everywhere I Roam. By Arnold Sundgaard and Marc Connelly. No record of copyright and no known extant copy. Produced in New York, 1938.

The Land of the Living. Copyright ms., 1938, 102 typed pp., is only known manuscript. Revised and retitled, *There Are Two Points.* Copyright ms., 1952, 101 typed pp., is only known manuscript. Produced in London, as *Hunter's Moon,* 1952. No known extant copy under that title.

The Mole on Lincoln's Cheek. In James Boyd, ed. *The Free Company Presents ... A Collection of Plays About the Meaning of America.* New York: Dodd, Mead and Company, 1941.

The Flowers of Virtue. Copyright ms., January 10, 1945, 137 typed pp., is only known manuscript.

A Story for Strangers. A fantasy. Copyright ms., January 5, 1948, 118 typed pp., is only known manuscript.

The Spring. Screenplay. "Based on *Gouverneur de la Rosee,* by Jacques Roumain." Copyrighted, 1953. Mr. Connelly's personal ms., 72 typed pp., is only known manuscript.

The Riddle. Motion picture play. Copyright ms., not dated, c. 1954, 94 typed pp., is only known manuscript.

Hunter's Moon. Produced 1958. See *Land of the Living,* above.

The Portable Yenberry. Comedy. Copyright ms., January 6, 1961, is only known manuscript of original script, but Mr. Connelly has been revising this play with the intention of a New York opening.

2. *Fiction* (Listed Chronologically)

"Luncheon at Sea." *New Yorker,* III (July 9, 1927), 18–19. Satire of Rotary Club luncheons.

"Gentleman Returning from a Party." *New Yorker,* III (November 19, 1927), 24–25.

"Barmecide's Feast." *New Yorker,* III (December 24, 1927), 13–15. In *New Yorker Scrapbook.* New York: Doubleday, Doran & Co., Inc., 1931; and *Short Stories from The New Yorker.* New York: Simon & Schuster, 1940.

"Fable." *New Yorker*, IV (March 3, 1928), 23–24. Medieval romantic tale.
"A Dear Old Couple." *New Yorker*, IV (March 24, 1928), 19–20. In *New Yorker Scrapbook.*
"The Committee: A Study of Contemporary New York Life." *New Yorker*, IV (April 7, 1928), 22–24. Story in skit form.
"An Hour Before High Noon." *New Yorker*, IV (April 21, 1928), 23–25. Companion piece to "The Bridegroom."
"The Guest." *New Yorker*, V (December 21, 1929), 23–24. In Robert N. Linscott. *Comic Relief: An Omnibus of Modern American Humor.* New York: Blue Ribbon Books, 1942; and Robert N. Linscott. *Best American Humorous Short Stories.* New York: Random House, 1945.
"Coroner's Inquest." *Colliers Magazine*, LXXXV (February 8, 1930), 23–24. In James D. McCullum, ed. *College Omnibus.* New York: Harcourt, Brace and Company, 1933; Charles D. Grayson, ed. *Half-a-Hundred Tales by Great American Writers.* New York: Garden City Publishing Company, 1945; Ellery Queen, ed. (pseud.). *To the Queen's Taste.* New York: Little, Brown and Company, 1946; and A. P. Blaustein, ed. *Fiction Goes to Court.* New York: Holt, 1954.
A Souvenir from Qam. New York: Holt, Rinehart, and Winston, 1965.

3. *Essays and Miscellaneous* (Listed Chronologically)

"Jots and Tittles." Pittsburgh *Gazette Times*, 1914 and 1915. Sunday column of comments, short jests, and verse.
"Redhead With Something Under It." *Everybody's Magazine*, XLIV (January, 1921), 19–20. Short, appreciative biography of Irene Franklin, the actress.
"Sideline Interpolations." In H. T. Webster's *Poker Book.* New York: Simon and Schuster, 1926.
"Washington in a Sack Suit." *New Yorker*, III (March 5, 1927), 28. Light satire on President Coolidge's speech about Washington as a "practical business man."
"Paris, 1927 Style." *New Yorker*, III (June 4, 1927), 60–61. Good-natured satire of Paris as a tourist trap.
"Profile: A Boy in a Barn." *New Yorker*, IV (March 31, 1928), 29–31. Appreciative essay about Joe Cook, the "One-Man Vaudeville Show," for whom Connelly wrote *How's The King?*.
"Prominent New Yorker: Major Fennister." *New Yorker*, IV (April 28, 1928), 21–22. Profile of democratic banker.
"A Panic in Hollywood." *New Yorker*, IV (July 28, 1928), 14–15. Satire on the effects of "talking pictures" on silent-screen actors.
"We're Going To Have Better Plays." *Theatre Magazine*, LII (December 30, 1930), 16, 62–64.
"The Life of the Theatre." *Saturday Review*, XXXVII (October 23, 1954), 13–14 and 40–43.
"A Curtain Rises." *New Yorker*, XXX (December 18, 1954), 120–27.
"June." *Saturday Review*, XXXVIII (January 1, 1955), 33.
"Warm Memoirs of Robert Benchley That Gay and Gallant Gentleman." New York *Herald Tribune*, November 13, 1955, Section 6, 1.

Selected Bibliography

"The Seven Seas: The Atlantic." *Saturday Review,* XLII (October 17, 1959), 30–32. Travel article.

"More About Ross" in "The Phoenix Nest." *Saturday Review,* XLII (October 17, 1959), 8. Letter about Harold Ross.

"The Long Foolishness." *New York: Sunday Herald Tribune Magazine,* December 8, 1963, 11–13. Essay about early days of Prohibition in New York.

"I Was a Septuagenarian Cub." *Variety,* July 18, 1964, 2 and 55. Unsympathetic account of 1964 Republican Convention.

"Benchley: My Most Unforgettable Character." *Reader's Digest,* LXXXVI (May, 1965), 72–78.

"Mayors, Moreno, and a Marriage." *Saturday Review,* L (January 7, 1967), 54–59.

SECONDARY SOURCES

I. *Biographical Materials*

(There is, at the present time, no biography of Marc Connelly. He is, however, listed in all of the standard biographical reference books for American authors.)

ADAMS, FRANKLIN P. (F.P.A.). *The Diary of Our Own Samuel Pepys.* 2 vols. New York: Simon and Schuster, 1935. Excellent for day-by-day accounts of Connelly's activities in the 1920's.

ALTSCHULER, HARRY. "A Novel Thing Just Happened," *World Telegram and Sun Feature Magazine Section,* June 12, 1965, 17. Excellent account of early years.

BARR, W. H. "McKeesport-Born Playwright, Famous For 'Green Pastures', Recalls Hair-breadth Escape From Death During Speedy Sled Ride In Jenny Lind Street," McKeesport *Daily News,* March 27, 1936, 1.

"City's Marc Connelly In Defenders Series," McKeesport *Daily News,* November 11, 1963, 4. Includes summary of career.

"Connelly In Quest For New Harrison," McKeesport *Daily News,* February 4, 1944, 1. Useful comments on *The Green Pastures.*

"Divine Comedian," *Time,* XLIX (May 19, 1947), 80. Review of career.

EATON, WALTER PRICHARD. "A Playboy Makes Good," New York *Herald Tribune,* March 23, 1930, Magazine Section, 10–12. Best single biographical sketch of Connelly in the 1920's.

"Famed Playwright Marc Connelly Recalls Childhood in McKeesport," McKeesport *Daily News,* July 5, 1964, 1, 8.

"Famous Native Son Captivates Audience with Views of Life, Theater, Early Days," McKeesport *Daily News,* January 27, 1965, 1. Good account of Connelly as public speaker.

HARRIMAN, MARGARET CASE. *The Vicious Circle: The Story of the Algonquin Round Table.* New York: Rinehart & Co., Inc., 1951. Good account of Connelly's early public life.

HYAMS, JOE. "Joe Hyams in Hollywood: Marc Connelly Previews a 'Script'," New York *Herald Tribune,* August 25, 1959, 24. Brief demonstration of Connelly's wit.

JANEWAY, MICHAEL. "Marc Connelly High on Happy Drama," *Newsday,*
August 1, 1963, 14. Review of a speech.

KELLEY, MARION. "Backstage: Marc Connelly Back with Prize Play," Phila-
delphia *Inquirer,* March 24, 1951, 21, 24.

KRAMER, DALE. *Ross and the New Yorker.* New York: Doubleday & Company, 1951. Few comments on Connelly's work.

MANTLE, BURNS. *American Playwrights of Today.* New York: Dodd, Mead
& Company, 1930. Brief, general account.

————. *Contemporary American Playwrights.* New York: Dodd, Mead &
Company, 1938. Brief, general account.

" 'Marc Connelly Day' Will Pay Tribute to Playwright," McKeesport *Daily
News,* December 12, 1966, 21. Review of career with special emphasis on
the uses that Connelly has made of McKeesport in his plays and novel.

"Marc Connelly Finds Self 'Starring' in New Medium," McKeesport *Daily
News,* November 16, 1966, 45. Review of his acting career with special
emphasis paid to his current activities on the lecture circuit.

McCRARY, TEX and JINX FALKENBURG. "New York Close-Up," New York
Herald Tribune, April 9, 1951, 24. Review of his activities in the 1920's.

MILLET, FRED B. *Contemporary American Authors.* New York: Harcourt,
Brace and Company, 1940. Factual account of his literary activities to
1934.

MOREHOUSE, WARD. "Broadway After Dark: 'Green Pastures'? ... Find the
Actor!," New York *Sun,* February 1, 1944, 20. Biographical account of his
career in the early 1940's.

————. "Broadway After Dark: Prof Connelly (Yale) Talks of 'Pastures',"
New York *Sun,* February 1, 1951, 20.

"On the Fringe: Answers from the Authors," *Saturday Review,* XLVIII (July
24, 1965), 40. Interview with Connelly.

OPPENHEIMER, GEORGE. *The Passionate Playgoer.* New York: Viking Press,
1958. S. J. Perelman's fanciful essay, "Arthur Kober," is of special interest.

"Sale for Chicago," *Newsweek,* XXIV (October 30, 1944), 22. Account of one
of Connelly's pranks.

"Some Playwright Biographies: ... Marc Connelly," *Theatre Arts Monthly,*
XI (July, 1927), 533–34.

THOMAS, BOB. "Connelly Confesses: I Was an Inner-Directed Under-Study,"
New York *World-Telegram and Sun Feature Magazine Section,* August
29, 1959, 4. Summary of his acting career.

WERSHBA, JOSEPH. "Daily Closeup: Marc Connelly," New York *Post,* March
5, 1959, 54. General Appreciative account of his various careers in theater.

WOOLLCOTT, ALEXANDER. *Enchanted Aisles.* New York: G. P. Putnam's Sons,
1924. Useful for view of Connelly as a member of the Thanatopsis
Literary and Straight Poker Society.

————. "Profiles: The Deep Tangled Kaufman," *New Yorker,* V (May 18,
1929), 26–29. Account of Connelly's playwriting activities through *The
Wisdom Tooth.*

————. "Two-Eyed Connelly," *New Yorker,* VI (April 12, 1930), 29–32. General
account of Connelly's early career.

Selected Bibliography

"Writer in Greasepaint," *Newsweek*, LIV (October 5, 1959), 27. Account of his activities in Hollywood.

II. *Critical Discussions*

(At the present time, the only work to discuss all of Connelly's plays—or even all the major ones—is this book. Probably the best single source for a running commentary on the major plays is Mantle's *Best Plays* series for those years in which Connelly's plays had New York openings.)

BROWN, JOHN MASON. *Upstage: The American Theatre in Performance.* New York: W. W. Norton & Co., Inc., 1930.

———. *Dramatis Personae.* New York: Viking Press, 1963. Excellent essay on *The Green Pastures.*

CARMER, CARL. "George Kaufman: Playmaker to Broadway," *Theatre Arts*, XVI (October, 1932), 159–68. Useful comments on those plays Kaufman did with Connelly.

CLARK, BARRETT H. and GEORGE FREEDLEY, eds. *A History of Modern Drama.* New York: Appleton-Century Crofts, 1947. Brief account of Connelly's work in the drama.

FLEXNER, ELEANOR. *American Playwrights: 1918–1938.* New York: Simon and Schuster, 1938. Brief account of Connelly.

GRIFFIN, ALICE and JOHN. "Satire in the New York Theatre," *Satire Newsletter*, II (Fall, 1964), 41–46. Connelly mentioned.

HEWITT, BERNARD. *Theatre U. S. A.: 1668 to 1957.* New York: McGraw-Hill Book Company, Inc., 1959. Includes reviews of *Dulcy, Beggar on Horseback,* and *The Green Pastures.*

HUGHES, GLENN. *History of American Theatre, 1700–1950.* New York: Samuel French, 1951. Sketchy account, including comment on *A Story for Strangers.*

ISAACS, EDITH J. R. *The Negro in the American Theatre.* New York: Theatre Arts, Inc., 1946. Useful account of *The Green Pastures.*

KRUTCH, JOSEPH WOOD. *American Drama Since 1918.* New York: George Braziller, Inc., 1957. A few, useful comments.

LEMBKE, R. W. "The George S. Kaufman Plays as Social History," *Quarterly Journal of Speech*, XXXIII (January, 1934), 76–84. Includes plays Kaufman wrote with Connelly.

QUINN, ARTHUR HOBSON. *History of the American Drama from the Civil War to the Present Day,* II. New York: Harper & Brothers, 1927. One of the few serious attempts by an academic critic to deal with the plays as literature.

SHIPLEY, JOSEPH T. *Guide to Great Plays.* Washington, D.C.: Public Affairs Press, 1956. Accounts of *Beggar on Horseback* and *The Green Pastures.*

SOBEL, BERNARD. "Musical Comedy, Quo Vadis?," *Theatre Arts Monthly*, XII (August, 1928), 566–75. A few, brief comments on the musical comedies he wrote with Kaufman.

ZOLOTOW, MAURICE. *Stagestruck: The Romance of Alfred Lunt and Lynn Fontanne.* New York: Harcourt, Brace & World, Inc., 1965. Theatrical account of *Dulcy.*

III. *Selected Reviews and Discussions of Individual Works*

Beggar on Horseback

KELLOCK, H. "Beggar on Horseback," *Freeman,* VIII (March 5, 1924), 617–18. Short, favorable review.

LEWISOHN, LOUIS. "Beggar on Horseback," *Nation,* CXVIII (February 27, 1924), 238–39. Largely a summary of play.

MACGOWAN, KENNETH. "From the Four Corners of American Art," *Theatre Arts,* VIII (April, 1924), 215–28. Brief Mention.

YOUNG, STARK. "Beggar on Horseback," *New Republic,* XXXVIII (March 5, 1924), 45–46. Favorable, impressionistic essay.

Dulcy

HACKETT, F. "Dulcy," *New Republic,* XXVIII (August 31, 1921), 28. Short, favorable review.

Everywhere I Roam

BROWN, JOHN MASON. "Two on the Aisle: Mr. Connelly and Mr. Blau Stage 'Everywhere I Roam'," New York *Post,* January 8, 1939, 6. Generally unfavorable review.

"New Plays in Manhattan," *Time,* XXXIII (January 9, 1939), 25. An attack upon social philosophy of play.

WYATT, EUPHEMIA VAN RENSSELAER. "Americana," *Catholic World,* CXLV (February, 1939), 597. Review comment.

The Farmer Takes a Wife

WYATT, EUPHEMIA VAN RENSSELAER. "The Farmer Takes a Wife," *Catholic World,* CXL (December, 1934), 340. Favorable review.

The Flowers of Virtue

FREEDLEY, GEORGE. "The Stage Today: Marc Connelly's 'Flowers of Virtue' Has Many Bright, Humorous Spots," New York *Morning Telegraph,* February 6, 1942, 22. Largely favorable review.

The Green Pastures

ATKINSON, BROOKS. "The Green Pastures," New York *Times,* February 27, 1930, 23; reprinted in Montrose J. Moses and John Mason Brown, eds. *The American Theatre.* New York: W. W. Norton & Co., 1954, pp. 278–81. Favorable account of play and its intent.

CARMER, CARL. "The Green Pastures," *Theatre Arts,* XIV (October, 1930), 897–98. Favorable review.

FERGUSSON, FRANCIS. " 'The Green Pastures' Revisited," *Bookman,* LXXIII (May, 1931), 194–95. Favorable review.

FORD, NICK AARON. "How Genuine Is the Green Pastures?," *Phylon,* XX (Spring, 1960), 67–70. Unfavorable review.

HUTCHENS, JOHN. "The Black Miracle: Broadway in Review," *Theatre Arts,* XIV (May, 1930), 369–77; reprinted in *Theatre Arts Anthology.* New York: Theatre Arts Books, 1950. Favorable account of play.

Selected Bibliography

KRUMPLEMANN, JOHN T. "Marc Connelly's *The Green Pastures* and Goethe's *Faust*," *Studies in Comparative Literature*, VII (Fall, 1962), 199–218. Study shows likenesses.

NOLAN, PAUL T. "God on Stage: A Problem in Characterization; Marc Connelly's *Green Pastures*," *Xavier University Studies*, IV (May, 1965), 75–84. Argues for humanistic reading of play.

———. "Marc Connelly's 'Divine Comedy'; *Green Pastures* Revisited," *Western Speech*, XXX (Fall, 1966), 216–24.

SKINNER, R. DANA. "*The Green Pastures*," in Moses and Brown, *American Theatre*, above, pp. 278–91. Favorable review.

STEINER, E. A. "Fashion Play of 1930: Green Pastures and the Oberammergau Passion Play," *Christian Century*, XLVII (August 13, 1930), 985. Appreciation of religious intent.

THOMPSON, ALAN REYNOLDS. "A Varied Shelf," *Bookman*, XXXI (June, 1930), 340–41. Short, descriptive account.

WILKINGTON, ROBERT. "Note on the Corpus Christi Plays and 'The Green Pastures'," *Shakespeare Association Bulletin*, IX (Fall, 1934), 173–97. Morality elements in play.

WOOLLCOTT, ALEXANDER. "Shouts and Murmurs, 'The Green Pastures," *New Yorker*, VI (March 22, 1930), 34. Defense of play.

YOUNG, STARK. "The Green Pastures," *New Republic*, LXII (March 19, 1930), 128–29. Favorable review.

A Souvenir from Qam

"Dewdrop Man," *Newsweek*, LXV (June 18, 1965), 88. Brief mention.

DOLBIER, MAURICE. "A Novel Failure for a Playwright," New York *Herald Tribune*, June 7, 1965, 24. Unfavorable review.

"Oil in the Garden of Eden," *Atlantic Monthly*, CCXVI (September, 1965), 145. Mildly favorable review.

A Story for Strangers

GIBBS, WOLCOTT. "Just Louder, Not Funny," *New Yorker*, XXIV (October 2, 1948), 49–52. Unfavorable review.

KRUTCH, JOSEPH WOOD. "Drama," *Nation*, CLVII (October 2, 1948), 381. Harshly critical review of play and direction.

PHELAN, KAPPO (pseud.). "The Stage & Screen: *A Story for Strangers*," *Commonweal*, XLIII (October 8, 1948), 618.

"The Theater," *Time*, LII (October 4, 1948), 59. Brief satiric comment.

The Wild Man of Borneo

BROWN, JOHN MASON. "The Dull Devil of Melodrama: Broadway in Review," *Theatre Arts*, XI (November, 1927), 812–26. Not altogether unfavorable, but objects to parts.

YOUNG, STARK. "Wild Men," *New Republic*, LII (September 28, 1927), 148–49. Generally favorable review.

The Wisdom Tooth

YOUNG, STARK. "The Wisdom Tooth," *New Republic*, XLVI (March 3, 1926), 45. Favorable review.

IV. *General*

DOWNER, ALAN S. *Fifty Years of American Drama, 1900–50*. Chicago: Henry Regnery, 1951. Useful for general background.

GAGEY, EDMOND M. *Revolution in American Drama*. New York: Columbia University Press, 1947. Connelly mentioned briefly.

HART, MOSS. *Act One: An Autobiography*. New York: Random House, 1959. Useful for view of Connelly's first collaborator.

HIMELSTEIN, MORGAN Y. *Drama Was a Weapon: The Left–Wing Theatre in New York 1929–1941*. New Brunswick, New Jersey: Rutgers University Press, 1963. Only Connelly play mentioned is *Everywhere I Roam*.

KNIGHT, ARTHUR. *The Liveliest Art*. New York: Macmillan Company, 1957. Good background for Connelly's film work.

LANGER, LAWRENCE. *The Magic Curtain*. New York: E. P. Dutton & Company, Inc., 1951. Langer: ". . . disdained . . . the general chitchat . . . in which many of the Round Table members indulged themselves," but the "Algonquin crowd . . . made a brilliant contribution, both critical and creative. . . ."

MOREHOUSE, WARD. *Forty-five Minutes Past Eight*. New York: Dial Press, 1929. Good insights into Broadway theater.

O'HARA, FRANK HURBURT. *Today in American Drama*. Chicago: University of Chicago Press, 1939. General account.

ROBKIN, GERALD. *Drama and Commitment: Politics in the American Theatre of the Thirties*. Bloomington: Indiana University Press, 1964. Only a few passing references to Connelly's plays.

SELDES, GILBERT. *The Seven Lively Arts*. New York: Harper & Brothers, 1924. Useful for background on film work.

WEALES, GERALD. *American Drama Since World War II*. New York: Harcourt, Brace & World, Inc., 1962. Useful as a typical view of Connelly's work of the past twenty years: "Marc Connelly, whose output has always been small, had one unsuccessful play on Broadway—*A Story for Strangers*."

WILDE, PERCIVAL. *The Craftsmanship of the The One-Act Play*. New York: Crown Publishers, Inc., 1951. Favorable mention of *Little David*.

Index

Index

Index